LISTENING TO THE SPIRIT
IN THE TEXT

Listening to the Spirit in the Text

GORDON D. FEE

WILLIAM B. EERDMANS PUBLISHING COMPANY
GRAND RAPIDS, MICHIGAN / CAMBRIDGE, U.K.

REGENT COLLEGE PUBLISHING
VANCOUVER, BRITISH COLUMBIA

© 2000 Wm. B. Eerdmans Publishing Co.
All rights reserved

This volume published jointly by
Wm. B. Eerdmans Publishing Co.
255 Jefferson Ave. S.E., Grand Rapids, Michigan 49503 /
P.O. Box 163, Cambridge CB3 9PU U.K.
www. eerdmans.com
and by
Regent College Publishing
an imprint of Regent College Bookstore
5800 University Boulevard, Vancouver, B.C. V6T 2E4

Printed in the United States of America

05 04 03 02 01 00   7 6 5 4 3 2 1

Library of Congress Cataloging-in-Publication Data

Fee, Gordon D.
    Listening to the spirit in the text / Gordon D. Fee.
        p.   cm.
    ISBN 0-8028-4757-9 (pbk.: alk. paper)
        1. Spiritual life — Biblical teaching.   2. Church — Biblical teaching.   I. Title.

BS680.S7 F44 2000
230'.04115 — dc21

                                              00-041730

Contents

Contents

Author's Preface

Some explanation is needed about this collection of essays, only one of which (chapter 8) appears in print here for the first time. The origin of the collection reflects what is true about most of the essays as well: they were gathered at the instigation of friends at Regent College and Eerdmans Publishing Company, who thought there might be some value for them to reach a broader audience. So also most of them were written by invitation of some kind, which often provided an opportunity to put into writing some matters that I had been reflecting on for myself.

These essays have two things in common. First, they tend to reflect my interests in Pauline studies and especially in the role of the Spirit in Paul's own spiritual life and in that of his churches. The first chapter gets at the very heart of things for me: that the Spirituality of the biblical text should be part of our historical investigation — and obedience — as New Testament exegetes. Second, in contrast to much of my work, the essays were not written with the New Testament guild or professional clergy in view, but for a much broader audience. Indeed, six of them appeared first in *Crux*, whose subtitle is "A Quarterly Journal of Christian Thought and Opinion published by Regent College." Along with chapter 8, which was a Regent College Summer School lecture in July 1997, five of them were prepared first for oral presentation (chs. 1, 3, 6, 10, 11), which only later were presented for publication; and in some of these cases I resisted revising them too much from their original oral form.

I also resisted making any substantive changes to these essays from their original printed form. Together these various factors mean that (1) there is a degree of unevenness about them, (2) there is a degree of inevitable repetition, and (3) there are sometimes oblique references to other people or works that are not footnoted. With regard to the second point, this is especially true about my deep concern to rescue the word "spiritual" (and therefore "spirituality") — especially with reference to Paul's usage — from its various meanings in English that all stem from a Greek worldview that has absolutely nothing to do with Paul. With regard to the third point, I need to note especially the references in chapter 6 to essays by my three Regent colleagues, Maxine Hancock, Iain Provan, and Rikki Watts. Their three lectures preceded mine in a Regent College Winter School course on gender issues and also appear with mine in the same issue of *Crux*.

I need to thank two former Regent College students, Rob Clements (who edits Regent College Bookcentre publications) and Mike Thomson (a former Teaching Assistant, who is now Sales Director for Eerdmans), for their initiative in seeing this project through to publication. I also need to thank Eerdmans for their willingness to publish these essays and for letting them remain in their original form, since they are of such a different genre from my other Eerdmans publications (commentaries on 1 Corinthians and Philippians, and a collection of essays [with Eldon J. Epp] on New Testament textual criticism).

Finally, a word of thanks to other publishers/publications (Hendrickson Publishers, InterVarsity Press, *Crux, New Oxford Review, Theology Today, Journal of the Evangelical Theological Society*) for permission to reprint these essays here. The original publication data:

Chapter 1: *Crux* 31/4 (1995), 29-35.
Chapter 2: *Theology Today* 46 (1990), 387-92.
Chapter 3: *Crux* 28/2 (1992), 2-5.
Chapter 4: *Alive to God: Studies in Spirituality presented to James Houston*
(ed. J. I. Packer and L. Wilkinson; Downers Grove: InterVarsity, 1992), 96-107.

Chapter 5: *New Oxford Review* 48 (May 1981), 8-11.
Chapter 6: *Crux* 35/2 (1999), 34-45.
Chapter 7: *Crux* 29/4 (1993), 34-39.
Chapter 9: *Crux* 31/1 (1995), 22-31.
Chapter 10: *Crux* 25/4 (1989), 3-13.
Chapter 11: *Journal of the Evangelical Theological Society* 28 (1985), 141-51.
Chapter 12: *Called and Empowered: Pentecostal Perspectives on Global Mission* (ed. M. W. Dempster, B. D. Klaus, D. Petersen; Peabody MA: Hendrickson, 1991), 7-21.

GORDON D. FEE

THE TEXT AND THE LIFE
IN THE SPIRIT

Chapter 1

Exegesis and Spirituality: Completing the Circle

Although the subject matter of this essay has been brewing over a long season, its present impetus stems from writing the commentary on Paul's letter to the Philippians during Winter and Spring of 1994. As I worked through Paul's text with great care, I experienced an ongoing encounter with the living God — Father, Son, and Holy Spirit — an encounter which happened in two ways. On the one hand, as I exegeted the text so as to articulate its meaning for the sake of others in the church, I was often myself so overcome by the power of the Word that I was brought to tears, to joy, to prayer, or to praise. On the other hand, I was also regularly experiencing the text of this letter in church settings, in such overwhelming ways, that I felt compelled to mention it in the final paragraph of the Author's Preface:

This essay was the first of four lectures delivered as the Ongman lectures at Örebro Theological Seminary, Örebro, Sweden, in December 1994, and repeated in slightly altered form as the Huber Drumwright lectures at the Southwestern Baptist Theological Seminary in October 1995. I have deliberately kept the lecture format and have resisted the temptation to add footnotes.

3

The writing of this commentary is unlike anything I have heretofore experienced as a part of the church. In a regular stream of divine appointments, in a variety of church settings over the four and a half months in which I wrote the first draft of the commentary, one Sunday after another either the worship (including liturgy) or the sermon was in some very direct way associated with the text of the preceding week. It was as though the Lord was letting me hear the passage played back in liturgical and homiletical settings that made me pause yet one more time and "hear" it in new ways. It is hard to describe these experiences, which had a profound impact on my sabbaths during the sabbatical; and their regularity seemed beyond mere coincidence. All of which made my Mondays take on a regular pattern as well, as I would go back to the prior week's work and think and pray it through yet one more time.

This essay was born out of these experiences. What I propose to examine is the interface between exegesis and spirituality, between the historical exercise of digging out the original intent of the text and the experience of hearing the text in the present in terms of both its presupposed and intentional spirituality. Thus I will attempt to address three matters: first, a few words about spirituality; second, some words about exegesis; and finally, some suggestions as to how these two must interface in order for us to be interpreting Scripture properly *on its own terms.*

These two topics, it should be noted, are very often perceived as being unrelated. Indeed, in most theological seminaries, one can take courses in exegesis, but "spirituality," that most slippery of words to pin down, is pretty much left to the individual — and there is seldom any suggestion that the latter has very much to do with the former. Indeed, even at Regent College, where we have faculty who teach in both disciplines, our students tend to take courses that focus on one or the other, and they are sometimes left with the impression that exegesis and spirituality are separate disciplines — which indeed they are academically. My concern is that they must somehow be brought much closer together or the ultimate aim of exegesis itself is lost.

4

I. SPIRITUALITY

I begin with a singular and passionate conviction: that the proper aim of all true theology is doxology. Theology that does not begin and end in worship is not biblical at all, but is rather the product of western philosophy. In the same way, I want to insist that the ultimate aim of all true exegesis is spirituality, in some form or another. And I insist on this because of my conviction that only when exegesis is so understood has the exegetical task been done in a way that is faithful to the intent of the text itself.

So let me address myself at the outset to the most difficult task of all — to offer a definition of "spirituality." As the result of my work on the *pneuma* ("Spirit") word group in the letters of Paul, I have found myself becoming more and more distressed by our translating the adjective *pneumatikos* with a small-case letter, "spiritual." Indeed, the word "spiritual" is an "accordion" word; its meaning pretty much has to do with how much air you pump in or out of it. The point that needs to be made is that the word *pneumatikos*, a distinctively Pauline word in the New Testament, has the Holy Spirit as its primary referent. Paul never uses it as an adjective referring to the human spirit; and whatever else, it is not an adjective that sets some *unseen* reality in contrast, for example, to something material, secular, ritual, or tangible.

In the New Testament, therefore, spirituality is defined altogether in terms of the Spirit of God (or Christ). One is spiritual to the degree that one lives in and walks by the Spirit; in Scripture the word has no other meaning, and no other measurement. Thus, when Paul says that "the Law is spiritual," he means that the Law belongs to the sphere of the Spirit (inspired of the Spirit as it is), not to the sphere of flesh. And this, despite how the flesh has taken advantage of the Law, since, even though the Law came through the Spirit, it was not accompanied by the *gift* of the Spirit so as to make it work in the hearts of God's people. So also, when Paul says to the Corinthians (14:27), "if any of you thinks he or she is spiritual," he means, "if any of you think of yourselves as a Spirit person, a person living the life of the Spirit." And when he says to the Galatians (6:1) that "those who are spiritual should restore one who has been overtaken in a transgression," he is not referring to some special or elitist group in the church, but to the rest of the believing community, who both began their life in the Spirit and come to completion by the same Spirit who produces his own fruit in their lives.

Thus in the New Testament, Christian existence is Trinitarian at its very roots. At the beginning and end of all things is the eternal God himself, to whom both Jews and Christians refer over and again as the Living God. God's purposes in creating beings like ourselves, fashioned in his image, was for the purposes of relationship — that we might live in fellowship with the Living God, as those who both bear his likeness and carry out his purposes on earth. From even before the fall, we are told that God had set about his purpose to redeem the fallen so as to reshape their now misshapen vision of God and thus to restore them into the fellowship from which they fell in their rebellion. God has brought this about, we are told, by himself coming among us in the person of his Son, who at one point in our human history effected our redemption and reconciliation with the Living God, through a humiliating death and glorious resurrection. But he has not left us on our own to make a go of it; he has purposed to come to our aid — and this is the reason for his coming to us and among us by his Holy Spirit.

Thus God's aim in our lives is "Spiritual" in this sense, that we, redeemed by the death of Christ, might be empowered by his Spirit both "to will and to do for the sake of his own pleasure." True spirituality, therefore, is nothing more nor less than life by the Spirit. "Having been brought to life by the Spirit," Paul tells the Galatians, "let us behave in ways that are in keeping with the Spirit."

Hence the aim of exegesis: to produce in our lives and the lives of others true Spirituality, in which God's people live in fellowship with the eternal and living God, and thus in keeping with God's own purposes in the world. But in order to do that effectively, true "Spirituality" must precede exegesis as well as flow from it.

Thus, I regularly tell students: Have the touch of God on your life. Live in fellowship with him; be among those who cry out with the Psalmist, "my soul and my flesh long for you"; "O God, you are my God; earnestly I seek you. My soul thirsts for you; my body longs for you, in a dry and weary land where there is no water." If those who teach and preach God's Word, which preaching must be based on solid exegesis of the text, do not themselves yearn for God, live constantly in God's presence, hunger and thirst after God — then how can they possibly bring off the ultimate goal of exegesis, to help to fashion God's people into genuine Spirituality?

Indeed, I don't much care what you call it — this touch of God on your life — but have it. Because without the presence and power of the Holy Spirit, all else is mere exercise — mere beating the air. To be a good exegete, and consequently a good theologian, one must know the fullness of the Spirit; and that includes a life of prayer ("praying in the Spirit," Paul calls it) and obedience.

A great danger lurks here, you understand, especially for those who have been called of God to serve the church in pastoral and teaching roles. The danger is to become a professional (in the pejorative sense of that word): to analyze texts and to talk *about* God, but slowly to let the fire of passion *for* God run low, so that one does not spend much time talking *with* God. I fear for students the day when exegesis becomes easy; or when exegesis is what one does primarily for the sake of others. Because all too often such exegesis is no longer accompanied with a burning heart, so that one no longer lets the texts speak to them. If the biblical text does not grip or possess one's own soul, it will likely do very little for those who hear.

All of this to say, then, that the first place that exegesis and Spirituality interface is in the exegete's own soul — that the aim of exegesis is Spirituality, which must be what the exegete brings to the exegetical task, as well as being the ultimate aim of the task itself. Such an understanding, I would argue, must belong to the exegetical task itself, to which we now turn.

II. EXEGESIS

It is not my intent here to describe good exegetical method. I assume one knows that exegesis consists of asking the right questions of the text, that those questions are basically of two kinds — contextual and content — that the contextual questions are also of two kinds (literary and historical) and that the content questions are four (de-

7

termining the original text, the meaning of words, the implications of grammar, and the historical-cultural background). My concern in this essay, rather, is to take up the question of how all this relates to the ultimate goal of Spirituality.

At issue here is finding the way between the two sirens that lurk on either side, that would woo the exegete toward one extreme or the other. The sirens are exegetical methodology (Scylla, if you will), on the one side, and a popular view of spirituality (Charybdis), on the other.

These two (exegetical method and spirituality) are seen as constantly at war with one another, with the result that piety in the church is — for good reason — highly suspicious of the scholar or the seminary-trained pastor, who seems forever to be telling people that the text does not mean what it seems plainly to say. The result is a reaction to good method as such, since such a way of looking at the text seems to run at cross-purposes with a more devotional reading of the Bible, where "the Word for the day" is received by one's direct encounter with the text in a more free-floating, associative way of reading texts. The bottom line is that such people take their own brand of "common sense" approach to the Bible: read it in a straightforward manner and apply it as you can; and "spiritualize" (sometimes = allegorize) the rest.

Came along the exegete and said "no" to such piety. Taking Scripture away from the believing community, the exegete made it an object of historical investigation. Armed with the so-called historical-critical method, he thus engaged in an exercise in history, pure and simple, an exercise that appeared all too often to begin from a stance of doubt — indeed, sometimes of historical skepticism with an anti-supernatural bias. Using professional jargon about form, redaction, and rhetorical criticism, the exegete, full of arrogance and assuming a stance of mastery over the text, often seemed to turn the text on its head so that it no longer spoke to the believing community as the powerful word of the living God.

The natural result of this bifurcation between church and academy has been suspicion on both sides, and much too often poor exegesis on the one side and almost no Spirituality on the other.

Partly at issue in this conflict is the role of history and authorial intentionality. Exegesis by definition means that one is seeking an author's own intent in what has been written. Such a definition implies that authors are intentional and that good historical investigation can provide a reasonable approximation of that intent. This means, therefore, that the exegetical task is first of all a historical one, and that the first requirement to do good exegesis is to bring good historical sense to the task. This further means that "meaning" is located primarily in intentionality, the author's intentionality. For the believing scholar, this means further that God's Word is very closely tied to the intentionality of the divinely inspired author.

It is common these days to reject this view of the exegetical task, a rejection that comes from several quarters besides the pious who read the text as a direct revelation to themselves: deconstructionism doubts whether there is any significance to such a task at all; reader-response criticism argues that more attention ought to be given to the text as text, and how the text is "heard" by the reader; and we are constantly reminded from all sides, (1) that one can never fully enter into the skull of another so as to know that person's mind — indeed, it is sometimes asked, did they know their own minds, or were they writing with unspoken agendas in hand that also affected what they said? and (2) that neither does the exegete come to the text with a clean slate, but also brings his or her agendas to the text, not to mention a whole train load of cultural baggage and biases.

Deconstructionism aside, I accept these as proper cautions to our exegetical task. But I also am prepared to repeat with emphasis, that authors are intentional, and that meaning resides ultimately in that intent. After all, everyone of those who argue against me at this point are very intentional in their writing, and would (rightly so) take great exception to me if I were to misconstrue their words in the same way they seem willing to treat the words of the biblical writer. My guide here is the Apostle Paul himself, who in writing to the church in Corinth took considerable exception to the Corinthians' misunderstanding — more likely, misconstruing — what he believed to be straightforward intentionality in his previous letter. I refer, of course, to 1 Corinthians 5:9-10: "I wrote to you in my letter not to associate with immoral people," which apparently they took to mean (i.e., that Paul *intended*) that they should not associate with people outside the church who were immoral. But Paul will have none of that, so he qualifies with an explanation of his own intentionality: "not at all meaning the people of this world who are immoral, greedy, etc." So also with his "not that" in Philippians 3:12, which Paul uses to qualify what he has just said. "In saying this," he now qualifies, "I do not mean. . . ." Therefore, let me say it again, authors are intentional, and since most authors also have at least normal egos, they do not take kindly to being misquoted, misinterpreted, or misconstrued — and all of that in light of what they understand to have been their own intentionality.

I am wont at this point to remind us all that various forms of intentionality are inherent in different literary genres and rhetorical features; that poetry, for example, is not prose, and that each has a different form of intent; or that prose is not all of one kind, and therefore that letters have a different kind of intent (depending on their type) from narrative or aphorisms; or that rhetoric sometimes involves an author in hyperbole, word plays, or metaphors, each of which has its own form of intent. When we speak of "intentionality," therefore, we understand that to include the form/style/genre in which an author purposes to communicate.

But having made that point, let me carry it a step further, which will also lead us to our final point: the intersection of exegesis and spirituality in the task of exegesis itself. Rather than seeing exegesis and spirituality as opposed to one another, or as one preceding or following or having precedence over the other, I propose, (1) that faithful biblical exegesis belongs within the framework of the believing community, with those who follow — whether exactly so or not, but intentionally so — in the train of the original believing communities for whom and to whom these documents were written; and, (2) that such exegesis must always take into account the Spiritual purposes for which the biblical documents were written, as Spirituality has been defined in the preceding section of this paper.

III. EXEGESIS AND SPIRITUALITY

In at least one point, those who fear the scholar exegete have it right, namely in their protest that the exegete tends to make Scripture a matter of history pure and simple, and then, often, to be skeptical of that history as well. I want to say with great vigor that even though the *first* task of the exegete is the historical one (= to determine the biblical author's intended meaning), this first task is *not* the *ultimate* one. The ultimate task, and now I repeat myself, is the Spiritual one, to hear the text in such a way that it leads the reader/hearer into the worship of God and into conformity to God and his ways. My present point is that this task is not to be separated from the historical one, or added onto it at the end. Rather, determining the Spiritual intent of the text, as we have previously defined Spirituality, belongs legitimately — indeed, necessarily — to the historical task itself.

I do not mean by this that what is often termed application or devotion is to be understood as part of the exegetical task itself. Rather, I mean that the biblical authors to a person were not only inspired by the Holy Spirit — or so we believe — but also brought their own Spirituality to their writing of the text. My point is that true exegesis attempts to engage in the author's *Spirituality*, not just in his or her words. Moreover, our engagement at this level is not to be a merely descriptive task (as in, "Paul was a passionate lover of Christ"), but a genuinely empathetic one, so that we ourselves become passionate lovers of Christ if we are to hear the text on Paul's terms and not simply on our own.

Of what earthly or eternal value is it, for example, for us to exegete Philippians 1:21 ("for to me to live is Christ, to die is gain"), in purely descriptive terms, if we do not engage in Paul's further intent that the Philippians themselves share this view of present life? It is easy to point out the place of this text in its context, that Paul is picking up on the two possible resolutions of his imprisonment, freedom or execution, and offers a brief personal reflection as to what either of them means for him. We can go on to describe the rhetorical power of the assonance, which would have caused the Philippians to have heard these words in ways we cannot, and to suggest further in light of what we know elsewhere from Paul that this statement registers as a kind of motto for his life. Indeed, we might even go beyond that to try to catch something of Paul's Spirituality, and thus to comment, for example (and now from the commentary):

> As he puts it in 3:12-14, having been "apprehended by Christ Jesus," Christ thus became the singular pursuit of his life. "Christ" — crucified, exalted Lord, present by the Spirit, coming king; "Christ," the one who as God "emptied himself" and as man "humbled himself" — to death on the cross — whom God has now given the name above all names (2:6-11); "Christ," the one for whom he has gladly "suffered the loss of all things" in order to "gain" him and "know" him, both his resurrection power and participation in his sufferings (3:7-11); "Christ," the name that sums up for Paul the whole range of his new relationship to God: personal devotion, commitment, service, the gospel, ministry, communion, inspiration — everything.

But what is the point of such description if we do not press on to ask further about Paul's intent what he was expecting the *Philippians* to do with such a statement? And what does it mean further for us *as the heirs of their text* to be brought up short in the face of this text with our own mottoes which seem to fall so far short of this one (e.g., "for to me to live is to be honored by colleagues and students"). But unless we do so, unless we are encountered by Paul's own Spirituality, have we truly engaged in the ultimate exegetical task? Because these words are not simply an autobiographical aphorism; these words are intended to call the Philippians — and us — to the imitation of Paul.

The Apostle makes this abundantly clear in 4:9: "What things you have learned or received or heard or seen in me, practice these things." True Spirituality, life in the Spirit, is precisely the aim of all that Paul writes to them; and this is precisely where the "imitatio" motif, which figures largely in many of Paul's letters and arguably dominates Philippians from beginning to end, fits into his view of things. His readers are urged to imitate him, to follow his cruciform lifestyle as depicted in his own story in 3:4-14, just as his story is closely related to the Christ story in 2:5-11. At issue in Philippi is their need to have the same mindset regarding the gospel, and to live with one another in the kind of humility that puts the needs and interests of each other ahead of one's own. They are thus urged to have the same mindset as Christ, who as God, demonstrated God's true character by pouring himself out and taking the form of a slave, and who as man humbled himself by becoming obedient to death, even death on the cross. But they are further urged to imitate Paul, whose own story finds its focal point in "knowing Christ Jesus my Lord," which is further clarified as simultaneously knowing the power of his resurrection, as he also participates in Christ's suffering, so as to be conformed to Christ's likeness in his death. And those who live otherwise, he goes on to say in 3:18-19, whose minds are on present, earthly things, are thus enemies of the cross. To hear this letter aright we must be prepared to imitate Paul in his cruciform lifestyle, as his own life was an imitation of Christ's pouring himself out for the sake of others, even to the point of death on the cross.

And that leads me to my final concern about the Spiritual intent of this motif in Philippians. Paul understood Christian life and discipleship quite in contrast to our own Spirituality, in which we are quite content to put the Bible into people's hands but would not think of telling them to follow our example as we follow Christ. Part of our excuse for this, of course, is that we have a perfectionist's view of the world, that if we are not ourselves perfect then we should never suggest that others follow our example. But Paul is quite ready to say that he has not yet arrived at the full completion of his knowledge of Christ (3:12-14), but he will urge them to follow his example in any case. I would suggest that we have not entered into the full Spirituality of these texts until we are ready to follow Christ so fully that we can tell those whom we have been given to teach that they should mark our lives, and the lives of those who walk as we do, and thus follow our example. We are not talking about being perfect, of course, but about having a mindset like Christ's, so that through the power of his resurrection our lives are lived so as to be in conformity to his death. When we have so set our own minds, and behave accordingly, and urge others to follow us in this way, then we might have something truly to say to our broken and fallen world.

I would urge that good exegesis and true Spirituality should meet at precisely this point in our interpretation of Philippians.

Finally, I would argue, if we do not go on to this step of the process, that is, if our exegesis and spirituality do not join hand to hand at *this* point, then I wonder whether what we do may rightly be called *biblical* exegesis. To put all of this in another way — and in contemporary terms: Because we believe Scripture is God's Word, by which God addresses us, that means that Scripture is the subject and we are the object. During the process of exegesis we momentarily reverse these roles, so that we act as subject with the text as object. I would argue that the exegetical process is not completed until we return to the proper posture of objects being addressed by the subject.

IV. A CONCLUDING NOTE

But all has not been said. Let us assume for the moment that what I have urged in this essay is right, that true exegesis has not taken place until we have closed the circle and entered into the intended Spirituality of the text. The obvious next question is: So how do we do that? What do we do as exegetes, as interpreters of the Word, so as to do both the historical and Spiritual task well, so that they blend in our lives and are not viewed as two separate disciplines?

1. The key is to be found in one's overall stance toward Scripture, from beginning to end. This includes several things, but at least it means to come to the text with an absolute conviction that it is *God's* word; that here God speaks and we listen. Thus our concern in coming to the text is to hear from God. No other stance is exegetically in keeping with the text itself.

Such a stance also includes a conviction that the text has been inspired by the Holy Spirit; for only with such a conviction will one expect the same Holy Spirit to help us in the twofold task of being good historians and good listeners.

2. The second key lies with our concern to do good exegesis, to hear the text first on *its* own terms, not *our* own. This, of course, stands over against a popular notion of Spirituality, which believes that learning gets in the way of hearing the text in a spiritual way.

But such an approach to the text misunderstands the biblical meaning of Spirituality. And very often such an approach to the text gives one warm feelings about the biblical text and about God, but it does not always lead to obedience or to being encountered by God's own purposes in giving us the text in the first place.

In contrast to such a view, I urge that true Spirituality demands that we do our exegesis as carefully as our skills and opportunities make it possible. Since everyone who reads the text also interprets as one reads, the question is not whether one will do exegesis or not — everyone will and does — but whether one will do *good* exegesis or not.

The reason we must learn to do good exegesis is precisely because we are passionate to hear and obey. This means that we must also be passionate to get it right regarding the meaning of the text — not that God is waiting for our exegesis before he can speak to the church, but because if the text is going to lead us to genuinely biblical Spirituality, we must have the text right so as to have our Spirituality conform to the intent of the text.

3. Which leads me, third, to suggest that our exegesis, therefore, must be kept in the context of the believing community. We must learn to hear the text together, to let the exegetical expert work hard on the text, but to insist that what he or she has learned in the privacy of one's study must be tested in the believing community. For the true heirs of the Philippians, who first received this text, are not the scholars who have objectified the text and made it their own, but the community of believers who are committed to listening to God and walking in his ways.

4. Which leads me finally back to the beginning. Our final stance toward the text must be that with which we began; but it now must be informed by an exegesis that has completed the circle. And such completion takes place truly only when we rise up and follow, when we who would be "spiritual" recognize that true spirituality is not simply inward devotion but worship that evidences itself in obedience and the same kind of God-likeness we have seen in Christ himself.

This, then, is what I think exegesis and spirituality are all about: not separate, or separated, disciplines, but one discipline that requires us simultaneously to be good historians — that is, good students of the Word — and good pray-ers.

Chapter 2

Reflections on Commentary Writing

I would think myself to be the least likely person ever to have written a commentary. While this reflects a degree of insecurity on my part (why would anyone care to read what I had written?), more significantly it reflects a longstanding concern as to what a good commentary ought to look like — not to mention whether I could ever bring it off.

Not only have I regularly had to use commentaries (gladly so, but often with frustration), but as a seminary professor I am regularly asked to recommend the "best" commentary(-ies) to others. Over the years, I had come to some provisional conclusions about what I thought should go into a good commentary, and finally I built up enough courage (integrity?) to give it a try for myself (under the rubric, "those who live in glass houses," etc.). Whether I have succeeded in satisfying the needs of others remains to be seen, but at least I can set forth what motivated me to engage in this folly that someone has called "the least creative of all scholarly art forms."

First, a demurrer. I do not in fact consider most commentaries bad, although their degree of usefulness is often dictated by the parameters of a series (and free-standing commentaries are usually less than successful). But to find all the features that I look for in a single commentary is not easy. Five faults come to mind: expounding the obvious while skirting the difficult; erring on the side of "ex-

16

position" without paying adequate attention to exegetical details (textual issues, lexicography, grammar); its opposite, expounding on the nuance of every preposition or participle without an adequate exposition of the text; engaging in a running debate with scholarship without adequately engaging in conversation with the biblical author; and expounding verses seriatim without adequate discussion of the historical and literary contexts.

When I accepted the invitation to write the commentary on the Pastoral Epistles (PE) in the Good News Commentary series (Harper & Row, but now revised as the New International Biblical Commentary, Hendrickson), I knew the limitations of the series would mean an exposition without enough space either to discuss points of detail or to interact adequately with scholarship. As a friend put it, "I liked your conclusions, but it would have been helpful to see how you arrived at them." Nonetheless, there is a place for such a commentary, especially for the inquiring lay person (always hoping, of course, that pastors might find the exposition itself useful to their purposes).

On the other hand, the offer (which in this case I initiated) to replace Grosheide's considerably outdated commentary on 1 Corinthians in the NICNT series gave me the opportunity I was looking for. I was fortunate that both the editor of the series (F. F. Bruce) and the copy-editor at Eerdmans (Milton Essenburg) were congenial toward some slight modifications of the format of the series, so that I could indulge most of my personal interests. Moreover, between the writing of the PE commentary and that on 1 Corinthians, I experienced the ultimate personal quantum leap of learning to use a word processor. The PE commentary was written in long hand and passed through four full stages of typing, plus galleys and page proofs; 1 Corinthians was submitted both in hard copy (1800 pages of typescript) and disk, and went directly from copy-editing to page proofs.

I was held up for a long time at the beginning trying to decide on which translation to use as the basis for comment. Editorial policy for replacement volumes allowed me to abandon the ASV of the first volumes and either to create my own or to use anything else available. I had long determined not to create my own, since I thought the reader ought to have the advantage of a Bible in common with others. My own choice boiled down to the RSV, NASB, and NIV. In some ways the sheer woodenness of the NASB would have made it an excellent basis for comment, but I finally settled on the NIV mostly because I thought it to be the most common translation among those who constitute the greater market for the series — but also partly because of some dissatisfaction with the RSV on 7:25 and the NASB on 7:36-38 (plus the fact that Professor Bruce had written his New Century commentary on the RSV). As I began to work my way through the text I also came to be a bit disillusioned with the NIV and finally secured permission from Zondervan Publishers to alter its text in several places where I found it exegetically impossible or, in many cases, where it employed unnecessarily sexist language. Although I tend to favor dynamic equivalence as a translational theory, both commentaries (the first was originally written against the GNB) have given me reason to pause. For my own tastes I found far too many absolutely wrong exegetical choices now locked into the biblical text as the reader's only option.

I began the actual writing by experimenting with several paragraphs in 1 Corinthians 1, until I had satisfied myself on several counts: First, I was driven by the desire to offer a readable exposition of the text, as uncluttered by technical jargon and other commentary paraphernalia as I could possibly make it. Reviews and personal letters have indicated that there has been a measure of success, the secret to which for me was the word processor. Every morning I ran off hard copy of the previous day's (sometimes days') work and read it aloud in its entirety, including footnotes. Every time I stumbled over a sentence, or had to catch my breath, I assumed another reader would also have difficulty; so I rewrote until I felt it read aloud smoothly. I also read the entire product through aloud one final time before submitting it to Eerdmans; not all the bugs are out, but I am convinced this has been the key to what measure of readability it might have.

Second, my greatest disappointment with most commentaries has been what I felt to be an inadequate placement of any given text into its historical and literary context. I was determined that whatever else, this commentary would be the opposite — so much so that

I could easily be accused of overdoing it. I chose to introduce each major section in terms of its relationship to the historical situation in Corinth; then, in keeping with the series format, each paragraph received its own discussion, but in this case with a considerable introduction that tried to do three things: (1) show how the paragraph related to what had been said to this point; (2) show how it in turn advanced the argument; and (3) overview the argument of the paragraph itself so that the reader could see how Paul's thinking proceeded. I then tried to do the same for each verse, always beginning with a word as to how it fitted into what had preceded and how it functioned in the argument before taking up the various pieces of the sentence seriatim.

The greatest difficulty I had at this point was to determine what belonged in the body of the text and what should be relegated to footnotes. Certain criteria emerged early on. Some things automatically belonged in the notes, including most technical discussions of the Greek text (especially textual criticism and grammar) as well as almost all interactions with scholarship. On all other matters, the decision was made on the basis of the two criteria of a readable exposition and the significance of the issue for understanding what Paul had said. The interchange of matter between text and notes continued right up to the final draft.

Third, I was also concerned that Paul's own theological urgencies get their proper hearing. From my perspective, it has been a blight on the landscape of much New Testament scholarship probably related to our twin concerns to affirm pluralism and not to offend others — that we have been good technicians of the text, but have avoided theology like the plague. It is hard to imagine anything less fair to Paul himself, who was an intensely theological person. So for good or ill, I wanted Paul's theological emphases, as I perceived them, to get their full hearing. Whether I have understood the Apostle adequately remains for others to judge, but surely one fails to comment adequately on Paul who does not try to "hear" him, to come to grips with what drives him, what motivates the words and the rhetoric.

Finally, and I wrestled long and hard with this one, I decided to conclude the discussion of each paragraph with some hermeneutical observations, either as to its overall theological import or how it might apply. My nervousness here stemmed not only from my awareness that such things simply are not done (scholarship seems almost to be embarrassed by belief), but by the obvious pitfalls of such an undertaking, namely, the danger that such comments might become too quickly dated, or otherwise too parochial or local; the possibility of being overly simplistic (which in fact was suggested by one reviewer); or that I might be doing for others what they should be doing for themselves.

On the other hand, two things made me willing to give it a try. First, I have taught this letter for so many years in seminary and church settings, where hermeneutical issues are always the greater urgency, that it seemed a matter of personal integrity to wrestle with these issues again in the commentary itself. Second, it seemed to me to be in keeping with the aim of the series not only to offer an exposition of the text, but also to give some hints as to how it might apply to our own setting. I have no illusions as to whether everything is either right on or helpful to others, but I have spent years wrestling with the matters of application and it seemed appropriate to offer some suggestions that might serve as a point of departure for a pastor's own thinking since the commentary is aimed primarily for her or him. In fact, there has been far more favorable reaction to this dimension of the commentary than I had dared hope.

Although not all will be convinced, I do hope to have cut new ground at several points. On some smaller details, I would like to think I have resolved an issue regarding the grammar on 4:6 and 7:7. I also have given a more elaborate case than can be found heretofore for "flesh" = "sinful nature" in 5:5, and as far as I know I am the only commentator to eliminate 14:34-35 on textual grounds alone. I hope to have made more significant contributions, or at least to have opened paths for new discussion, on my overall view of the letter as basically one of conflict between Paul and the church over the matter of what it means to be "spiritual," on the historical issue lying behind chapters 8–10, and on 11:2-16 as reflecting a breakdown between the sexes, not the subordination of women.

This latter text is one of several in this letter that should cause one to think twice before writing a commentary. It remains as one of the four places (along with 11:19, 12:3, and 15:29) where I am convinced that none of us really knows what the text means. The problem with writing a commentary, of course, as over against teaching a course, is that in the latter one can more easily glide over some things that the writing of a commentary will not allow. The personal *Angst* comes from the realization that these are some of the first places to which others will turn in opening the commentary and then judge the whole by these.

On the more personal side, several things stand out. First, I continually wrestled with the personal struggle between writing a commentary for scholars or for the church in a more direct way (pastors and students). There were two events that kept me honest (in favor of the church more directly). The first of these is to be found in the dedication to a longtime friend Wayne Kraiss, who became president of Southern California College several years after I had left there for Wheaton and then on to Gordon-Conwell. We were both in a conference for church leaders at Arrowhead Springs, where I was doing some things from 1 Corinthians. In a passing moment, of those kinds where one has to make a personal transition because the time is getting away, I commented that I had the contract to write a commentary on this letter, but did not have sabbatical time coming in which to do it. The next day Wayne asked me how long it would take to write it if I could get a leave of absence (the answer: an academic year with summers on either side). It turned out that there was a special fund at the college, directed and disbursed by a committee of which he was chair. The result was an offer from my former institution of a full year's salary, with absolutely no strings attached (I am not used to the church acting in this way; it has given me new hope), to take a leave of absence from Gordon-Conwell, because, as Wayne put it to me, "the church needs that commentary." Whether that was so or not, those words always came ringing back in my ears whenever I started to get carried away in the body of the exposition with some long, involved argument with scholarship over some detail.

The other event was equally significant. On a Sunday morning early on in the writing, a member of my local assembly, Bob McManus, stood during prayer time and said that he felt led of the

Holy Spirit to pray for me during the time that I was writing the commentary and invited others to join him. The result was a group of about ten people who each took a day of the week, committing themselves to prayer for me, and to whom I "reported in" once a month. I simply cannot describe how significant this became for me. I recall many a moment when I was starting to go astray after scholarship or when the muse ceased, or I was simply stuck at one of the difficult texts — when the awareness that some friends were in prayer for this enterprise caused the logjam to burst and direction and purpose to return. My gratitude and indebtedness to them for reminding me in this very tangible way of the ministry of the body to its own can never be fully expressed.

Finally, I must mention the several times when I had very personal encounters with the living God through the power of the text itself. These, of course, are very personal, but they were gentle reminders from the Holy Spirit that this is God's Word after all, and that God will have the final say, not I. Such encounters shine through at several places, such as 1:18-25, 4:7, 14:33, to name a few I clearly remember.

One of the more remarkable of these moments came with 4:9-13, commenting on Paul's hardship list, which served for him both to set forth his own apostolic ministry as in keeping with the gospel of the Crucified One and to offer the Corinthians a model for themselves. I was simply overcome with the dissonance of my sitting in the comfort of my study, with my word processor and surrounded by my books, while trying to comment on these hardships as Paul's own norm for apostolic existence. It was not a matter of false guilt, but an overwhelming sense of my need, and that of those around me, to take stock of our lifestyles and values.

Perhaps for me the single most significant of these moments came at 13:4. One must first appreciate the kind of dread with which I finally came to these verses (13:4-7). Here is a passage so well known, and so full of inherent power, that comment by me would seem to be both profane and pedestrian. But as I began to reflect on the significance of the first two words on the list (longsuffering [KJV] and kindness), I was suddenly struck by the clear reality that these are two words that Paul elsewhere uses to describe the character of God (the passive and active sides of divine love). As I sat and reflected on what that meant, I was overwhelmed with an indescribable emotion, as it came to me that not only is God like this — eternally and faithfully so — but where would I be, and those I love, if it were not so. What if God loved with the same degree of longsuffering as I have toward those who have sinned against, or disappointed, me. It was one of those grand moments of hearing the gospel afresh and being renewed in the presence of God. It is also the kind of moment very difficult to capture in a commentary.

Much of the writing was simply hard work, keeping at it some twelve hours a day, six days a week, for fourteen months of actual writing. Along with the Sabbath, for which I came to have a new appreciation as God's gift to us, these moments of encounter with God through the text of the word were "seasons of refreshing." I only hope that something of my own love for this text and its power have shone through the commentary itself.

Chapter 3

On Being a Trinitarian Christian

At the conclusion of Paul's second canonical letter to Corinth, he signs off with what begins as a typical grace-benediction: "May the grace of our Lord Jesus Christ be with you all." But in this single instance in his preserved letters he elaborates that standard benediction by also invoking, besides the grace of Christ, the love of God and the fellowship of the Holy Spirit. The result is his well-known Trinitarian benediction, which, precisely because it is so well-known and often-used, is also so seldom reflected on:

> May the grace of our Lord Jesus Christ, and the love of God, and the fellowship of the Holy Spirit be with you all.

This benedictory prayer of Paul's is my own prayer — and most profound desire — for all of you, as you prepare to leave Regent — classes, friends, the Atrium, Footnotes* [a coffee bar] — and make your way into the marketplace into various forms of Christian service. My concern is that you leave Regent deeply committed to living as truly Trinitarian Christians, not simply in the theological sense of being able to affirm and perhaps even explicate this deepest mystery and most wonderful truth of our faith; but that you internalize, experience, and live out your faith in Trinitarian terms — as those whose whole lives are determined by, and thus lived in light of, the experience of God himself: God — Father, Son, and Holy Spirit.

My own experience with this text stems from a few days last July. As many of you know I have been working on a book on the Holy Spirit in the letters of Paul. I was nearing the end of the long chapter on 2 Corinthians. In a rather perfunctory way, I fear, and frankly in some haste to bring five weeks of writing on this Epistle to conclusion, I dashed off what seemed to be the obvious words that needed to be written about this text and put this part of the task to rest — or so I thought.

But the next morning I was awake very early. A day or two earlier Maudine and I had had conversation with a friend who was in especially deep need. Given the earliness of the hour, and the fact that nothing in my computer was particularly hot, I prepared to spend some extra time in prayer, especially for our friend. It was in that setting that the Spirit joined these two realities — our friend's need and this text of the day before — in what for me was one of those profoundly life-producing experiences with the living God. Needless to say, this part of the monograph also required a considerable rewriting.

This grace-benediction is so well known that it is easy for us to miss its several remarkable features: first, that Paul elaborates his concluding grace at all — which he does not do anywhere else, either in his earlier or later letters; second, that he does so with this Trinitarian formulation, which appears here in such a presuppositional way — not as something Paul argues for, but as the assumed, basic, experienced reality of Christian life. That it is in fact almost certainly an *ad hoc* elaboration, and not part of the church's existing liturgical tradition, seems certain by its third remarkable feature: the order — Christ, God, and Spirit, which can only be explained because Paul began his standard benediction, and then felt compelled to add words about the Father and the Spirit.

What came to me that morning, and obviously it had been percolating for months after working through so many Spirit texts in Paul, was that in many ways this benediction is the most profound theological moment in the Pauline corpus — in two ways:

First, it serves to encapsulate what lies at the very heart of all of

25

Paul's urgencies — the gospel, with its focus on salvation in Christ, equally available by faith to Gentile and Jew alike. The gospel is Paul's singular passion, and the gospel has to do with salvation — not simply salvation from sin, in the classical fundamentalist sense, but in the more profound biblical sense of God's purposes that began with creation and that will be consummated at Christ's coming — namely creating a people for his name, who will live in close relationship with him and will bear his likeness, and thus be for his glory. This text, therefore, in the form of prayer, encapsulates what is expressly stated in a large number of other passages (e.g., Rom 5:1-11; Gal 4:4-6; Eph 1:3-14), where we are told that God in love determined to create a people for his name, and in love took the initiative to bring it about. The "grace of our Lord Jesus Christ" is what gave concrete expression to that love; through Christ's suffering and death on behalf of his loved ones God effected salvation for them at one point in our human history. The "fellowship of the Holy Spirit" expresses the ongoing appropriation of that love and grace in the life of the believer and the believing community. This, therefore, is but one of some twenty or twenty-five texts, all of which speak to the heart of Paul's gospel, and in Trinitarian language — where God's love lies behind salvation, Christ's death and resurrection have effected salvation, and the Holy Spirit appropriates salvation to the life of the believer.

Second, this text also serves as our entrée into Paul's theology proper, that is, into his understanding of God himself, which had been so radically affected for him by the twin realities of the death and resurrection of Christ and the gift of the eschatological Spirit. In many ways I am a product of my discipline of New Testament studies, which tends to find this text something of an embarrassment. So much so, that whenever any of us talks about Paul's understanding of God, and the relationship of God and Christ, we are quick to demur — in the interests of the integrity of our discipline — that Paul was not a "Trinitarian" in the later sense, where the church was concerned — properly so — to work out how the one God could be three and still be one. I grant you that Paul did not wrestle with that ontological question, the question about God's being as such. But I am prepared to assert that Paul was fully Trinitarian in any meaningful sense of that term — that the one God is Father, Son, and Spirit, and that in dealing with Christ and the Spirit one is dealing with God every bit as much as one is with God the Father. As Karl Barth put it with great insight, "Trinity is the Christian name for God." And that understanding does not begin in the second or third centuries; it is already found in a most profound way with the Apostle Paul himself. I will contend with my discipline that with this elaboration, by its almost offhanded nature, we have the only legitimate starting point for Pauline theology.

With these words — words of prayer, I am quick to point out, which are always addressed to God — we begin to penetrate a bit into Paul's understanding of God, namely that to be Christian one must finally understand God in a Trinitarian way. Paul's understanding always begins with the Old Testament, which is thoroughly presuppositional for him. Whatever else may be said of God in the Old Testament, God's relationship with his people is primarily predicated on his love for them (Deut 7:7-8). This is what marks off the living God from all that is idolatrous surrounding Israel. What characterizes that love preeminently is his *hesed* (covenant love), which is usually translated "mercy" in the Septuagint. What Paul had come to see is that God's covenant love, so full of compassion and grace, has found its singularly concrete historical expression in the death and resurrection of Christ, which is expressed most powerfully in Paul in the familiar passage from Romans 5:1-5. And these are not mere words of ours. The certain evidence of God's love is that in Christ God himself became present "to reconcile the world unto himself" (2 Cor 5:20), and that that "love has been poured into our hearts by the Holy Spirit that has been given to us."

But that is not all, and this is where our Trinitarian understanding of God tends to break down. Through the gift of his Holy Spirit, the Spirit of the living God, God himself has now become present in the new creation as an abiding, empowering presence — so that what most characterizes the Holy Spirit is *koinonia*, a word that primarily means "participation in," or "fellowship with." This is how the living God not only brings us into an intimate and abiding relationship with himself, as the God of all grace, but also causes us to participate in all the benefits of that grace and salvation, indwelling us in the present by his own presence, guaranteeing our final eschatological glory.

Well, none of this is new to you. Whence my wonder that morning last July? Two things, both of which have to do with the Spirit. First, the Spirit that morning somehow helped me get past the mere factness of it all. These theological realities have been with me for life; and I have often been overawed by them. But somehow that morning I realized how little my friend — who also knows those realities, and got A's on papers in New Testament and theology — had truly internalized and appropriated them as the fundamental realities of her life. How I prayed for her — and pray now for you — that you may know the grace of our Lord Jesus Christ and the love of God and the fellowship of the Spirit, not simply as Christian truths, mere concepts that mark off the Christian faith from all others, but as the most truly profound and singular realities of the universe. So that all of life is lived out of this ultimate predicate of our existence — that God loves us, sinners all, and that we know that because Holy Week, culminating in Easter, and Pentecost are not simply yearly moments in the church's calendar, but are the fundamental realities of all human life.

But second, over the months, all kinds of Spirit texts were having their impact on me, and especially those in 2 Corinthians: such as 3:3-18, where the life-giving Spirit brings fulfillment to the old covenant — in the most remarkable way of all. As those who have had the veils removed from both our hearts and especially our faces, we by the Spirit not only behold God's own glory, seen in the face of Jesus Christ himself, but by the Spirit are also being transformed into that same likeness — from one measure of glory to another. Such texts were gripping my own soul. Here is the ultimate sharing in the Holy Spirit. By the Spirit, we are brought face to face with the living God and by the Spirit transformed into his likeness.

What came into clear focus, and experienced as reality that morning, is that I, and all believers like me, must forever be done with thinking of the Spirit in impersonal terms — as though the Spirit were an "it," some influence sent out from God, but short of being God, very God. For the meaning of the phrase "fellowship of the Holy Spirit," you see, does not so much refer to the Christian fellowship created by the Holy Spirit — as true and profound as that reality also is. Oh no, *koinonia* has to do with sharing in something, an actual participation in it. The Spirit is God's gift of the New Covenant whereby the covenantal promises of God's abiding and empowering presence in the lives of his people are being fulfilled.

And I began to think of my own Pentecostal heritage, and how we have depersonalized the Spirit — not in our theology itself, mind you, but in our ways of thinking and talking about the Spirit. Our speech is what betrays us. With us the Spirit is depersonalized into an empowering experience. We are empowered by the experience, but not by the empowering presence of God himself. And then I thought of my lifelong existence in evangelical circles — where the Spirit is kept safely in the creed and the liturgy. He is personal, well enough. We would be unorthodox to think otherwise. But for many, he is anything but God's empowering presence. Our images are biblical, but they are also impersonal. He is wind, fire, water — comes to us as influence, or whatever. But he is not the one in whom and by whom we are sharing in the very love and grace and life of God himself. And I do not mean in some mystical way. Our problem is that the language of Father and Son evoke personal images; but Spirit evokes that which is intangible, not quite real, because incorporeal. Paul's prayer, on the other hand, is that they might know the grace of Christ, the visible historical expression of the love of God, because as people of the Spirit they live in constant, empowering fellowship with God himself. This is how the loving God and the gracious Lord Jesus Christ are now present with us.

God's empowering presence — that is what "the fellowship of the Holy Spirit" means. God's empowering presence: That the Spirit is the way God has come to us in the present age, to be with us, to indwell us — both corporately and individually — to fellowship with us, and to empower us for life in the present as we await the consummation. By the Spirit our lives are invaded by the living God himself. God himself is present in and among us. This, too, is an Old Testament theme that for Paul finds fulfillment in Christ and the Spirit.

The theme begins in Genesis, in the Garden; the first result of the Fall was that the man and woman "hid themselves from the presence of God." The presence of God is the key to our understanding the book of Exodus, and the awesome events of Sinai. God was present on the Mount, first in the bush that burned but was not consumed, later in great and awesome displays of power, so that Israel could not go near. But Moses was brought up to the Mount to be in the presence of God. There he received not only the Book of the Covenant, but the directions for building the Tabernacle, by which God's presence was to leave the Mount, as it were, and accompany Israel. God's presence among them — this was to mark off God's people from the rest. But between the giving of the pattern for the Tabernacle, and its construction, there is the story of the debacle — Israel's eating and playing in the presence of a golden calf. The whole point of chapters 32–34 is God's readiness to wipe them out and start over. "You take them up," God says to Moses; "my presence will not go with them." "No," Moses prays, "if your Presence does not go with us, don't take us up from here, for how else will anyone know that we are your people, and that you are pleased with us, if your Presence does not go with us?" And God relents, and reveals himself to Moses in the awesome words of 34:6-7: "Yahweh, Yahweh, a God merciful and gracious, slow to anger, and abounding in steadfast love and faithfulness, keeping steadfast love for the thousandth generation, forgiving iniquity, transgression and sin, yet by no means clearing the guilty." Exodus then concludes with the construction of the Tabernacle, and the descent of God's glory — the evidence of his presence among them.

Later, in Solomon's Temple, where Exodus 40 is repeated, God's glory comes down again — God is now present with Israel in the Temple on Mount Zion. But there is continual failure in Israel, so finally Jeremiah prophesies that God will one day make a new covenant with his people, with Torah written on their hearts, which Ezekiel then picks up in terms of the Spirit. "I will put my Spirit within them," says the Lord through Ezekiel. "I will make breath (my Spirit) come into you and you shall come to life," he says to the dry bones. "Prophesy to the breath," God says to Ezekiel, "prophesy to the Spirit." "So I prophesied," says Ezekiel, "as he commanded me, and the Spirit entered into them, and they came to life — a vast army."

This, then, is what Paul understands by the gift of the eschatological Spirit. The Spirit of promise, he calls him, i.e., the promised Holy Spirit — the gift of God's own empowering presence. Thus, he pleads with the Corinthians, first corporately, then individually, "Do you not know that you, the church in Corinth, are God's temple in Corinth, and you are that because God's Spirit dwells in your midst?" "Do you not know," he pleads later in the context of their sexual sin, "that your bodies are the temples of the Holy Spirit, who dwells within you?" And again, in 2 Corinthians, to some who are still flirting with idolatry, he urges, using all of this rich imagery: "What fellowship is there between the temple of God and idols? For we are the temple of the living God. As God has said: 'I will live with them and walk among them, and I will be their God and they will be my people. . . . I will be a Father to you, and you will be my sons and daughters, says the Lord Almighty.'"

"Since we have these promises, dear friends," Paul concludes, "let us purify ourselves from everything that contaminates flesh and Spirit, perfecting holiness out of reverence for God." We ourselves, both individually and corporately, are the location of God's presence — by his Spirit. God himself — in the person of the Spirit — indwells us for fellowship with him, . . . and for life and service, as we are continually being transformed into God's own likeness by the indwelling Spirit.

And finally. The Spirit is not only God himself, present with us in fulfillment of his promises, but he is also an empowering presence — empowering us not only for gifts of building up the body as we worship in his presence, and for signs and wonders as part of that building up the body, but also for ministry and service in the world, and especially in Paul — for living in and boasting in our hope in the Lord Jesus Christ, even in the midst of — dare I say it in Paul's way — especially in the midst of weaknesses of all kinds. The grace of Christ is sufficient for us in the midst of suffering, conforming us to Christ's death even as we know the power of his resurrection — and all of this because we are the heirs of God through the new covenant as the result of God's unfailing love, demonstrated by the grace of our Lord Jesus Christ, and realized by the fellowship of the Holy Spirit.

Thus I pray for you, my dear graduating friends — earnestly, lovingly, and with great hope — first in the prayer with which Paul concludes his argument in Romans:

> May the God of hope fill you with all joy and peace in believing, so that you may abound in hope by the power of the Holy Spirit.

and then in the words of tonight's text:

> May the grace of our Lord Jesus Christ, and the love of God, and the fellowship of the Holy Spirit be with you all. Amen.

Chapter 4

Some Reflections on Pauline Spirituality

I t is a special privilege for me to offer the following reflections in honor of my esteemed colleague Jim Houston, whose life and teaching have been a constant reminder to us all that discipleship means to love God with one's whole being, not simply with one's head, as so often happens among theological academics. The subject of these reflections is one that is close to my own heart as well, since I am one Paulinist who thinks that the apostle has been poorly served in the church on this score. Paul is basically viewed and studied as either a theologian or a missionary evangelist, which of course are parts of the whole; but any careful reading of his letters will reveal that spirituality is crucial to his own life in Christ, as well as being the ultimate urgency of his ministry to others. Such a bold statement, of course, needs justification, which is what the following reflections are all about.

A LINGUISTIC NOTE

Failure to recognize the central role of spirituality in Paul stems at least in part from the use of the English word "spiritual" to translate the adjective πνευματικός in the Pauline letters.[1] This lower-case translation tends to obscure the fact that for Paul πνευματικός is primarily an adjective for the Spirit, referring to that which belongs to, or pertains to, the Spirit.[2]

Indeed, almost every non-Pauline understanding of the term "spiritual" can be traced to an inadequate English translation. Thus "spiritual" has been understood to mean religious (as over against either secular or mundane),[3] non-material/corporeal,[4] mystical,[5]

1. Even more unjustifiable is the translation of 1 Cor in the NIV, "he utters mysteries with his spirit" (where Paul clearly intends "he utters mysteries by the Spirit") or of 2 Tim 1:7 in the RSV and NIV, "For God did not give us a spirit of timidity, but a spirit of power, of love and of self-discipline" (where the context demands something like the GNB: "For the Spirit that God has given us does not make us timid; instead, his Spirit fills us with power, love, and self-control").

2. The word is almost an exclusively Pauline word in the New Testament, occurring 24 or 26 times in his letters, 15 times in 1 Corinthians alone. The adverb πνευματικῶς, which occurs in 1 Cor 2:14, also refers to the Spirit, meaning "discerned by means of the Spirit" (see G. D. Fee, *The First Epistle to the Corinthians* [Grand Rapids: Eerdmans, 1987], pp. 116-17).

3. The closest Paul comes to this concept is in Rom 15:27 and 1 Cor 9:11, where he speaks of the reciprocity between Christian service or ministry and receiving material benefits. He describes the former as "sharing/sowing τὰ πνευματικά [spiritual things]," but even here this choice of words has not to do with "spiritual" and "material," but with "the things of the Spirit" and material support.

4. This is often perceived to be the meaning of "spiritual body" in 1 Cor 15:44-46. But this contrast in particular is not between material and non-material, but between two *bodies,* one that belongs to our earthly existence, called ψυχικόν (= natural, of this present existence), the other that belongs to the heavenly sphere, the realm of the Spirit. It is still a "body," but is fitted for heavenly existence. Probably the best translation, therefore, is "supernatural" (as over against "natural"), or "heavenly" (as over against "earthly"). But it is not non-corporeal; it is a body, after all.

5. This meaning is especially read into the so-called "spiritual food and drink" problem of 1 Cor 10:3-4. But Paul's usage here has been called forth by the problem in Corinth itself, where they not only think of themselves as "spiritual" (almost certainly in a kind of triumphalist way over against Paul and his weaknesses) but as secured by the sacraments, which they apparently took to be evidence of their higher "spirituality." So Paul takes them on: the Israelites had their own form of "spiritual" food and drink, but it did most of them no good, since God was not pleased with them and overthrew them in the desert. Thus even here, in an indirect way to be sure, the adjective ultimately refers to the Spirit.

pertaining to the interior life of the believer,[6] or, in its worst moments, elitist (a spiritual Christian over against an everyday or carnal one).[7] But in fact not one of these meanings can be found either in Greek literature[8] or in Paul. For Paul "spiritual" in every case has some reference to the Spirit of God. Thus, for example, in Rom 1:11 he wants to impart some "spiritual gift" (= "gift of the Spirit"); in Col 1:9 he prays that they will be filled with all "spiritual wisdom and insight" (= "wisdom and insight from the Spirit"); in Col 3:16/ Eph 5:19 the "spiritual songs" are "songs inspired by the Spirit"; and the "spiritual blessings" of Eph 1:3 are "blessings that come from life in the Spirit."

Even more significant are those places where Paul refers to believers as πνευματικόι, where he clearly intends "people of the Spirit." The key Pauline passage in this regard is 1 Cor 2:6–3:1, which has had an unfortunate history of misinterpretation in the church.[9] Paul's point in context is a clear one. He is in the middle of an argument over against the Corinthians, who are into "wisdom," which they apparently consider to be their special gift of the Spirit, but which instead was full of all the overtones this word had in the Greek world. Against their "wisdom" Paul has argued in 1:18–2:5 that true wisdom, God's wisdom, stands in radical contradiction to that of the world, since it takes the form of a crucified Messiah, abject foolishness and weakness to merely human wisdom.

In 2:6-16, and with biting irony for those who think of themselves as "πνευματικοί" (Spirit people), Paul argues that in their by-

6. Theoretically this could be a possible meaning of the word, since Paul does use πνεῦμα a few times to refer to the interior expression of the human personality (cf. Rom 8:16, "the Spirit bears witness with our spirit"; 2 Cor 2:13, "I had no rest in my spirit"). But in fact in none of the 24 occurrences of πνευματικός does it refer to that which belongs to, or pertains to, the human spirit.

7. This usage is the result of both bad translations and unfortunate exegesis of 1 Cor 2:6–3:1. See the discussion below.

8. The closest thing to it is an obscure passage in Philo (*Rev. Div. Her.* 2.4.2); a bit later than Paul, Plutarch appears to use it to refer to the non-material side of human existence, but even this passage is disputed.

9. See n. 7 above. Almost every elitist, or deeper-life, brand of Christianity has found justification for its perspective in this passage, quite missing Paul's concern.

passing the cross for "wisdom" they have taken their place with the world, which in its wisdom "crucified the author of life"(!). With that he sets out in the starkest form possible the absolute contrast between believers and non-believers, those who have gone the way of God's wisdom and those who have not. The key to all of this is the Spirit, whom believers — including the Corinthians — have received. That the "foolishness of the cross" is God's wisdom has been revealed by the Spirit (v. 10); for only the Spirit of God knows the mind of God and has revealed it to us (v. 11). In receiving the Spirit, he goes on in v. 12, we did not receive that which makes us think like the world, but the Spirit of God himself, by whose presence in our lives we understand what God has graciously done in our behalf. Therefore (v. 13) what things we speak (about Christ crucified; cf. v. 2) are not in keeping with human wisdom but are taught us by the Spirit, which means that we explain "spiritual things" (i.e., "the things freely given us by the Spirit of God," v. 12) by "spiritual means" (i.e., "by means of the words taught by the Spirit").[10]

In contrast to us, who by the Spirit understand what God has been about in the cross, Paul continues in v. 14, there is the "ψυχικός person" (the person who is merely human, without the Spirit of God). Such a person does not receive the things of the Spirit of God — indeed, cannot know them — precisely because such things are discerned only by "spiritual" means (that is, by means of the Spirit). The one who is spiritual (the Spirit person), on the other hand, discerns all things (v. 15), precisely because by the Spirit we have received the mind of Christ (v. 16).

Then, with full irony, in 3:1-4 Paul presses his advantage. Even though they think of themselves — and in reality are — Spirit people, their thinking and behavior is that of non-Spirit people, so he has had to treat them accordingly — as mere babies. As long as there is quarreling and strife going on among them, Paul asks, are they not acting like mere human beings, that is, precisely like people who do not have the Spirit? The point of Paul's argument, of course, is "Stop it." My point is that for Paul what distinguishes believer from non-believer is the Spirit, pure and simple. God's people have the

10. On the meaning of this complex verse, see Fee, *1 Corinthians*, 114-15.

Spirit, and are by that very fact "spiritual" (= Spirit people), while others are not, nor can they be "spiritual" in any meaningful (for Paul) sense of that word, precisely because they lack the one thing necessary for "spiritual" life, the Spirit of the living God.

Paul uses πνευματκοί similarly in Gal 6:1. In a long argument (5:13–6:10) that Spirit people behave differently from those who are either in the flesh or under law, Paul concedes that even people of the Spirit from time to time may be "overtaken in a transgression" (6:1). Therefore, the rest of the believing community, as Spirit people, should restore such a one with the gentleness/meekness that is theirs by the Spirit.[11] All of this is to say, then, that for Paul "spirituality" is nothing more nor less than life in the Spirit, to which theme we now turn for a brief overview. Then we will look finally at what this meant for Paul's "spiritual" life, as we most commonly use this term, to refer to the life of prayer and devotion.

LIFE IN THE SPIRIT

Any careful reading of Paul's letters makes it abundantly clear that the Spirit is the key element, the *sine qua non,* of all Christian life and experience. To put that in theological perspective, it needs to be noted that, contrary to historic Protestantism, "justification by faith" is not the central theme of Pauline theology.[12] That is but one metaphor among many, and therefore much too narrow a view to capture the many-splendored richness of God's eschatological salvation that has been effected in Christ. For Paul the theme "salva-

---

11. Not "in a spirit of gentleness" (RSV) nor "gently" (NIV). The noun "gentleness" is precisely that noted in v. 23 as a fruit of the Spirit. Thus it is not "a spirit of" but "the Spirit who gives."

12. This theme in fact is only found in three of Paul's letters (Gal, Rom, Phil), and always in contexts where he is fighting against the imposition of Jewish "law," in the form of circumcision, upon his Gentile converts. This is not to downplay this metaphor, but simply to note that it is but one among several, all stemming from different ways of describing human fallenness (slavery to sin, hence "redemption"; under God's wrath, hence "propitiation"; alienated from God, hence "reconciliation"; etc.).

THE TEXT AND THE LIFE IN THE SPIRIT

tion in Christ" dominates everything, from beginning to end. And for him "salvation in Christ" is the activity of the triune God. God the Father, the subject of the saving verbs, has fore-ordained and initiated salvation for his people; God the Son, through his death on the cross, has effected it, and thereby accomplished for his people adoption, justification, redemption, sanctification, reconciliation, and propitiation, to name the primary metaphors. But it is God the Spirit who has effectively appropriated God's salvation in Christ in the life of the believer and of the believing community. Without the latter, the former simply does not happen.

Thus Gal 4:4-6: at the historically propitious moment God sent forth his Son to redeem, so that we might receive the full rights of sonship; and because "sonship" is what he had in mind he sent forth the Spirit of his Son into our hearts, who cries out "Abba, Father" to God. Similarly Titus 3:5-7: on the basis of sheer mercy, God saved us, through the washing of renewal and regeneration that come from the Spirit, whom he lavishly poured out on us through Christ, having justified us by the grace of Christ. And so it goes everywhere. Christ's saving act becomes an experienced reality through the gift of the Spirit of God, God's own personal presence in our human lives. Without the Spirit of God, one simply is not a part of the people of God.

So much is this so — that is, that Christian conversion is an experienced realization of God's own presence by his Spirit — that Paul writing to the Galatians appeals to this singular reality as the certain evidence that they do not need to succumb to Jewish boundary markers (Gal 3:2-5).[13] He wants to learn only one thing from them (v. 2), whether they received the Spirit by "works of law" or by "the hearing of faith." Since he has them on this one, he goes on to ask whether having begun by Spirit they intend now to come to comple-

13. The issue in Galatians is not first of all justification by faith (i.e, entrance requirements), but whether Gentiles who have already been justified by faith in Christ and given the Spirit must also submit to Jewish boundary markers (as Gen 17:1-14 makes so clear). For arguments presenting this perspective see T. David Gordon, "The Problem in Galatia," *Interpretation* 4 (1987); and J. D. Dunn, "The Theology of Galatians," *Society of Biblical Literature Seminar Papers* (Atlanta: Scholars Press, 1988), pp. 1-16.

tion by "flesh" (= circumcision). "Have you experienced[14] so much in vain?" he asks (v. 4). Finally, in v. 5 he appeals to their present experience of the Spirit: "He who supplies you with the Spirit and works miracles in your midst, does he do this by works of law or by the hearing of faith?"[15] The Spirit is the absolute key to everything, and the certain evidence that justification is by faith, not by doing works of law.

Not only so, but the whole of ongoing Christian life, both individual and corporate, is to be lived out in terms of the Spirit. The primary imperative for Paul, therefore, is "walk by the Spirit" (Gal 5:16); God's people are "led by the Spirit" (v. 18); their ethical life is described as bearing the fruit of the Spirit (vv. 22-23); and because, following the crucifixion of the flesh, they now live by means of the Spirit, they must behave in keeping with the Spirit (v. 25); they thereby sow and reap for and by the Spirit (6:8).

This, then, is what it means to be "spiritual" from Paul's point of view; it means to be a Spirit person, one whose whole life is full of, and lived out by, the power of the Spirit.

THE SPIRIT AND "SPIRITUAL" LIFE

But if what we have described above is how Paul basically understood "spirituality," it needs to be added that for him such Spirituality was also continuously "spiritual" in the sense of the word more common to us, that is, in a life of prayer and devotion. And it is this aspect of life in the Spirit that gets short shrift in traditional

---

14. The English versions have tended to translate ἐπάθετε, "suffered," in this passage (but see NEB, NRSV, Weymouth), on the legitimate linguistic grounds that this is the only meaning of the verb found elsewhere in Paul. But in fact the first meaning of the verb in Greek is simply "to experience." Since (1) there is not a hint elsewhere in this letter of "suffering" on the part of the Galatians, and (2) the context seems to cry out for the basic meaning of the verb here, this would seem to be Paul's clear intent. He is appealing to their having experienced so much of the Spirit's presence and activity in their midst.

15. One can only wonder in passing how such an argument would work in contemporary Christian churches!

Protestant theology, which tends to regard Paul basically as a thinker or a doer, rather than as a pray-er and a passionate lover of God.[16]

It is doubtful, of course, whether Paul would have easily recognized himself in our descriptions, nor would he have easily accommodated himself to our dichotomies. The gospel of Christ, which was the passion of his life, was not an abstraction to be thought about, but a reality to be proclaimed, experienced, and lived out, as one awaited its final consummation at the coming of our Lord. And it was to be lived out before God, and for one another.

Through Christ and the Spirit, God was now understood as a Father, and his people as brothers and sisters in the divine household, heirs of his glory because fellow-heirs with the eternal Son. Thus Paul's primary metaphors for the church (family, temple, body) all evoke images of the most intimate kind of bonding between believers and their Lord and with one another. This is the "participation in the Spirit" (or "fellowship of the Spirit") for which he prays in 2 Cor 13:13 and to which he appeals in Phil 2:1. When Paul could not be with a congregation in person, he understood himself to be present with them in the Spirit when they gathered together with the power and presence of the Lord Jesus (1 Cor 5:3-5; cf. Col 2:5) and read his letter.[17]

Such a bonding in the Spirit between the believer and his or her Lord and within the community led naturally to a life of continual prayer. Thus the apostle not only repeatedly prays for his brothers and sisters in Christ in his letters, but also regularly reports on such prayer, while frequently calling on his readers to pray for him and

16. The problem for us, of course, is that what we call "spirituality" is not something Paul wears on his sleeve. His letters are too *ad hoc,* too much aimed at correction or instruction, for him to reflect on his own personal piety. What we do learn comes to us from incidental moments, most often in passing, when he momentarily lifts the curtain of his private life. But such moments do occur, and since they are seldom the point of anything (thus not easily viewed as skewed by some other agenda), we need therefore to take them all the more seriously as reflecting the real life of the apostle as he himself lived in the Spirit.

17. On this text as having to do with Paul's real presence by the Spirit and not simply "with you in mind" see Fee, *1 Corinthians,* pp. 204-6.

others as well. My interest in this dimension of Paul's life in the Spirit, however, is not simply with the fact that he prayed continuously, but with the nature and form of that praying, because here, it seems to me, we get in touch with the real Paul in ways that conventional biblical theology seldom does, thereby missing a great deal.

Prayer as Rejoicing, Thanksgiving, Petition

In a series of concluding exhortations in his earliest letter, Paul urges the Thessalonians to "be joyful always, pray continuously, give thanks in all circumstances" (1 Thess 5:16); for, he adds, this is what God himself wills for them as they live out the life of Christ in Thessalonica. Most likely Paul is not talking about joy or thanksgiving in general; rather he is urging upon them life in the Spirit as a life of prayer. And prayer for him will naturally take the form of joy, praise, and thanksgiving, as well as petition.

Paul himself was as good as his imperative. Not too many months before this letter Paul and Silas were doing this very thing in the local jail in Philippi ("praying and singing hymns to God" [Acts 16:25] — in this case loudly enough for the rest of the jail to hear). So also earlier in this same letter (1 Thessalonians), Paul spoke thus of the return of Timothy: "How can we *thank* God enough for you in return for all the *joy* we have *in the presence of our God* because of you? Night and day we *pray* most earnestly that we may see you again . . ." (3:9-10). Some twelve years or so later, one finds this same collocation in his letter to Philippi (1:3-4, "I *thank* my God every time I remember you. In all my prayers for all of you, I *always pray with joy* because of your partnership in the gospel").

Continual prayer marked the apostle's life; but prayer was not simply petition for his congregations. First of all, prayer for them meant to be in remembrance of them; and remembrance of them was for him a cause of joy and thanksgiving. Thus he begins nearly every letter, frequently expressed in terms of "thanking God for [all of] you" — including the Corinthians, so many of whom stood over against him, as well as the Philippians and Thessalonians, his joy and crown. Thanksgiving had to do with people, not things or events; and the reason he could thank God for them all was precisely that they were all God's people, not his.

Two things about such continual thanksgiving and Paul's life in the Spirit need further theological reflection:

First, a life of continual thanksgiving — primarily in prayer, but to others for their generosity as well — is one of the certain signs of spiritual health (= a healthy life in the Spirit). It reflects a life that evidences the only proper posture before God — humility[18] — a life that is constantly aware of God's mercies, of living on the beneficiary side of life. Genuine thanksgiving stems from a grateful heart that has experienced truly what Paul asked the Corinthians rhetorically, "What have you that you have not received?" One can count on it as axiomatic — the diminution of thanksgiving in one's life is invariably accompanied by a concomitant increase of self-reliance and self-confidence. Gratitude is evidence of living under grace. Thus triumphalism is out, because life in the Spirit presupposes a life of prayer, which assumes a posture of humility before God and overflows with thanksgiving.

Second, that Paul's thanksgivings are most often expressed for people, not for things or events, is also evidence of spiritual health. Here is the key to genuinely sound relationships within the community of faith — to recognize others as gifts, as belonging first of all to God, no matter how nettlesome some of his gifts might seem to be to us. Thanking God for his people does not eliminate correcting or challenging them; Paul will still do that. But thanking God for them offers the possibility of reducing one's own self-importance in relationship to others. Here again, Paul models a kind of spirituality that we could well emulate. Whereas he came out fighting for the truth of the gospel — and his apostleship as it related to the gospel — Paul had the wonderful capacity to take himself as a person with hardly any seriousness at all (as Phil 1:12-26 offers marvelous evidence). When one lives as a truly free per-

---

18. In some expressions of the charismatic movement 1 Thess 5:18 has been used in a way that seemed to come very close to arrogance; continual praise was seen as a way of getting even more from God, as though God could be manipulated by our "praise" and "gratitude."

son before God, others have little or no control over one's life. And it is exactly that freedom that allows Paul always to give thanks to God for others who are his fellow-heirs in Christ (whether his converts or not, as in Colossians).

Because prayer begins as remembrance, evoking joy and thanksgiving in the Spirit, Paul therefore cannot help but petition God on their behalf as well. What is striking is the content of these petitions, which tend to take two expressions: a concern for their growth in the Lord, and a concern for the growth of the gospel. The latter concern, which sometimes includes a concern for deliverance from peril, is always front and center when he requests prayer *from them* in his behalf.[19] But in prayer *for them,* it is always that they might become Spirit people more and more, in terms of their own growth in grace. Thus in Col 1:9-11 he prays that they may know more of the Spirit's insight and wisdom, so that they might live worthy of Christ and be pleasing to him. To which he appends four participles that further define such a life: bearing fruit in every good work, growing in their knowledge of God (that is, coming to know his character the more), being strengthened by the power of the Spirit for endurance and patience, and joyfully giving thanks to the Father who has qualified them for their ultimate inheritance. One wonders whether it is possible to pray more significantly than this!

Thus prayer as rejoicing, thanksgiving, and petition marked Paul's own spirituality (life in the Spirit in terms of personal devotion), and was what he urged, and prayed, for his congregations. Paul was a pray-er *before* he was a doer or a thinker.

Prayer in the Spirit

One final matter central to prayer and Spirit needs to be noted, what Paul calls "prayer in the Spirit." Here is an especially sensitive area in Pauline spirituality that needs to be faced squarely both by New Testament scholarship and by the church at large, and not tip-

---

19. There is no content given in 1 Thess 5:25; but see 2 Thess 3:1-2 and Phil 1:19.

toed around because of generations of theological uneasiness or prejudice.

In Eph 6:18, in the context of spiritual warfare ("our struggle is not against flesh and blood, but against the rulers," etc.), Paul urges this congregation to "pray in the Spirit." Since this is the same language Paul uses about his own prayer habits in 1 Cor 14:13-16, one may legitimately assume that in using this language, at least one form such prayer would take would be praying "in a tongue." The argument in 1 Cor 14:1-19 gives clear evidence for the fact that praying in the Spirit, in tongues, held a significant place in Paul's own prayer life. Four texts are significant for our understanding this dimension of Pauline spirituality, three of which come from the argument in 1 Corinthians 14.

(1) 1 Cor 14:2. It is clear from the outset — and from the argument throughout — that Paul is trying to curb the practice (apparently highly regarded by the Corinthians themselves) of praying out in tongues without interpretation in the gathered community.[20] The concern of the argument throughout, as vv. 18-19 make certain, is what happens in the *community* at worship; and for Paul intelligibility is the key to edification when the church assembles. This is why Paul can offer such positive words about "tongues," while at the same time trying to curb it in the community, at least without interpretation. Thus in trying to stifle it as a community activity, he is careful not to quash it as a form of personal spirituality, precisely because it held a significant role in his own spiritual life.

The first word about "tongues" in this passage (14:2) is therefore both a positive one and one that sets what else he has to say in perspective. Here we learn two things about his understanding of this phenomenon. First, the person who "speaks in tongues" does not speak to people but to God. That is, such "speech" is obviously prayer speech. This is further confirmed by the explicit collocation of the verb "pray" with "in tongues" in v. 14, as well as by the implication in v. 28, let such a person "speak to himself [=privately] and God."

---

20. Very likely in this case he is also trying to curb its less than orderly expression, especially if, as 14:23 suggests and 14:27 implies, many of them were speaking out in tongues at the same time.

Second, such speech to God is not understood by the "mind" of the one praying. Rather "no one understands, but one by the Spirit speaks mysteries." For many in the West, of course, this is to damn Paul — and others who so speak to God — because only what passes through the cortex of the brain is allowed value in the age of enlightenment. Such "enlightenment," however, is simply the ultimate form of rationalism, where value is to be found only in what is "rational" (= having to do with the thinking processes) and where almost no value at all is given to the non-rational (indeed, it is often perceived as irrational).

But Paul and the early church had not been tampered with by the mind-set of rationalism, and he found great value in prayer that was from the heart, from within, but which did not necessarily need approval from the mind to be uttered before God. Indeed, in v. 4 Paul insists that such prayer is edifying to the one who so prays.

(2) 1 Cor 14:14-17. In this passage we are given yet further insight into prayer in the Spirit. By prayer and singing "with my spirit," Paul almost certainly means that the Holy Spirit prays through his own spirit.[21] Both the context and the explicit language of v. 14 demand that "praying in tongues" is what is in view. Two further matters are noteworthy.

First, Paul insists that he will do both, that is, he will pray and sing both with his understanding and in the Spirit, where his own understanding is not "fruitful." Whatever else, therefore, "prayer in the Spirit" is neither the most important nor the only kind of praying Paul will do. But it is obviously for him a part of the whole. What he disallows is such praying in the public assembly without interpretation, because it edifies only the speaker, not the others.

Second, vv. 16-17 indicate that such prayer in the Spirit may take the form of "blessing God" and "thanksgiving," which we have noted above is a key element in Paul's understanding of prayer.

(3) 1 Cor 14:18-19. Here is an unfortunately much abused text, which in fact lifts the curtain just a little, so that we may look in on Paul's own personal life of prayer. It is purely prejudicial, and an as-

---

21. Hence my suggested translation, "my S/spirit prays." See *1 Corinthians*, pp. 669-70.

sertion that should be forever laid to rest, that Paul is here "damning tongues with faint praise." How he could have known he prayed in tongues more than all of them is an irrelevancy. What is relevant is that Paul could make such an assertion to a community that so highly prized this gift as evidence of "heavenly spirituality." Had he not been able to justify the assertion, the entire argument comes aground. Probably to *their* own great surprise, he prizes their prize as well — but as having to do with "praying to himself" (v. 28, = in private), not in the congregation. In church he will only pray "with his mind," since congregational utterances, whatever form they take (i.e., to God or to others), must be intelligible so that the whole community can be edified. Otherwise, why gather; why not simply pray and sing only in private with no public expression of corporate worship? Thus this passage tells us that Paul can make a distinction between private and public prayer, and that in his own private prayer, he prayed in the Spirit more than all of them.

(4) Rom 8:26-27. Here is another much discussed text, especially as to whether or not it refers to "speaking in tongues."[22] Against such lie the facts (a) that Paul does not explicitly speak about "tongues," and (b) that the words στεναγμοῖς ἀλαλήτοις, "with groans that words cannot express," should properly mean "without words" or "unexpressed."

On the other hand, the parallels with 1 Corinthians 14 are equally striking: (a) as in 1 Cor 14:2 and 14-16, the Spirit prays (in this case, intercedes) through the believer; and (b) the believer who so prays by the Spirit does not necessarily understand what the Spirit is saying. Despite the words στεναγμοῖς ἀλαλήτοις, it is difficult to imagine this passage as arguing that there is no articulation in prayer; therefore, Paul probably means not so much that the words "cannot even be spoken," but that even though spoken they are inarticulate in the sense of not being understood by the speaker.

In any case, even if not referring directly to tongues as such, here is yet another text, appearing at a crucial point in an argument,

---

22. See the debate aroused by Käsemann's espousal of this text as referring directly to the same glossolalic phenomenon as in 1 Cor 14. For views that differ from what is suggested here, see the commentaries by Cranfield, Morris, and Dunn.

which gives certain evidence for a kind of praying in the Spirit that is not "praying with the mind."

All together these texts indicate that Pauline "spirituality" included, as an integral part, prayer that was Spirit-inspired and Spirit-uttered, which included both praise/thanksgiving to God and intercession (presumably on behalf of others as well as for oneself). This is not the only form of prayer for Paul, but it formed a significant part of prayer for him. All of which is but one more indication that for him, "spirituality," even in our sense of that term, was primarily "Spirit-uality."

A CONCLUDING POSTSCRIPT

Because of the way this paper is set up, it may appear as if my intent were to press for "tongues" as a necessary part of biblical spirituality. But such is not the case. I really intend these primarily as reflections. My first interest is with Paul himself. As one who has lived with the apostle through his letters over many years, I am convinced that his spiritual life, as much as can be seen through the thin curtains that tend to keep it hidden from us, is every bit as significant for our understanding of the man and his theology as is his "theology" itself and his apostolic ministry as an apostle to the Gentiles.

By this final section, however, I do intend that we cease looking at Paul only through the bifocals of our own Enlightenment-conditioned culture, and let him be his own person in the first-century church. What seems clear to me is that Paul simply cannot be understood apart from the central role the Spirit played in his own spiritual life, in his ministry, and in the life of his churches. To look at his "Spirit-uality" in this way not only will help us to appreciate biblical spirituality a bit more, but will, I hope, help us also to listen to Paul a bit more carefully — even a bit differently — as we try to hear him theologically.

I trust that such reflections, even if not fully agreed with, are in some measure in keeping with the concerns of my dear brother in Christ in whose honor they have been put to paper.

Chapter 5

The New Testament View
of Wealth and Possessions

H istorically the church has repeatedly had to wrestle with its existence as a pilgrim people in an alien, temporal society. This
has been true especially of its attitude toward wealth and material
goods. For the first two Christian centuries that struggle was relatively easy. Christians, by and large, stood over against culture on
this matter. When the emperor adopted the faith, however, the
struggle began in earnest. The monastic movement was one of the
direct results. Subsequent history has been an ebb and flow of accommodation and rejection. From time to time accommodation
has brought guilt, which in turn caused some to construct a theology for rejection, while others constructed a theology to justify
wholesale accommodation.

This historic struggle is currently an existential reality for American Christianity. In recent years the economic situation has in-
creased wealth for most Americans on a grand scale, producing considerable tension for large numbers of American Christians —
especially in light of the biblical mandate to care for the poor and
the fact that one and a half billion people in today's world are mal-
nourished. Most affluent American Christians have accommodated
rather easily to an affluent lifestyle, without giving it much

thought. Others have sensed the tremendous disparity between their affluent circumstances and the lowly Nazarene, whose perfect humanity is seen as a model for us, and have opted for a simpler way of life. Still others have begun to argue that affluence is God's intention — his perfect will for his children.

My interest in this essay is not to try to resolve these tensions for the individual Christian in modern American society. Rather it is my hope to indicate what the New Testament itself teaches about wealth and material goods, so as to provide a biblical frame of reference for discussion and decision making.

Anyone with even a surface acquaintance with the New Testament has come to recognize that the Christian faith is decidedly on the side of "the poor" and that "the rich" seem regularly to "come in for it." Thus Jesus says, "Blessed are you who are poor" and "woe to you who are rich" (Luke 6:20, 24, NIV). His messianic credentials are vindicated by the fact that "the good news is preached to the poor" (Matt 11:5; see Luke 4:18), while of the rich he says, "It is easier for a camel to go through the eye of a needle than for a rich man to enter the kingdom of God" (Mark 10:25). In his parable of the Sower he warns of "the deceitfulness of wealth and the desire for other things" that choke out the Word of God (Mark 4:19), while elsewhere he says that one cannot serve God and money — they are mutually exclusive masters (Matt 6:24).

Such an attitude toward wealth is reflected further in James and Paul, not to mention John's Revelation (18:16-17: "Woe, Woe, O great city, dressed in fine linen, purple and scarlet, and glittering with gold, precious stones and pearls! In one hour such great wealth has been brought to ruin"). James shames the church for showing favoritism to the rich (2:1-7) and especially in 5:1-6 condemns the rich for their oppression of the poor ("Now listen, you rich people, weep and wail because of the misery that is coming upon you"). And Paul warns that the rich who eat their "love feasts" and Lord's Supper without regard to the poor are coming under God's judgment (1 Cor 11:17-34); elsewhere he warns those who want to get rich that such people "fall into temptation and a trap and into many foolish and harmful desires that plunge people into ruin and destruction" (1 Tim 6:6-10).

In the light of such texts it is no wonder that affluent Christians sometimes experience guilt, as though wealth, or being wealthy, in itself were evil. But such is not the case. As we shall see, it is the abuse or accumulation of wealth while others are in need that is called into question.

It is possible of course, to argue — as some have — that these texts merely reflect the sociology of the early Christians, whose founder was a peasant carpenter, and whose early adherents were "not many wise, nor influential, nor of noble birth" (1 Cor 1:26) and who had sometimes experienced the confiscation of their property (Heb 10:34). Blessing the poor and condemning the rich was simply their form of making a virtue of necessity.

But such a sociological reading of the New Testament is a thorough misunderstanding of the deeply theological motivation of New Testament ethics, which ultimately derives from the Old Testament revelation of God as the One who Himself champions the cause of the poor.

It should be noted here that "the poor" in both the New and especially the Old Testaments, refers not merely to those in economic poverty. The "poor" are the powerless, the disenfranchised, those whose situation forces them to be dependent on the help of others. Thus it includes especially the widow and the orphan, as well as the alien, and even the Levite. The Old Testament Law, therefore, is filled with statutes that protect such people from the aggrandizement of the powerful, who of course are people with authority — and wealth.

Interestingly enough, it has been the Old Testament that has often been seen as the "balance" to the New with regard to personal wealth and prosperity. For here indeed one regularly finds prosperity (especially lands and children) as evidence of God's favor (e.g., Deut 28:14; Psa 112:1-3; 128:1-4). So much is this so that Sir Francis Bacon could write: "Prosperity is the blessing of the Old Testament; adversity is the blessing of the New."

But what is often overlooked in such texts is that they are invariably tied to the concepts of God's righteousness and justice. It is only as one is righteous — i.e., walks in accordance with God's Law — that one is promised the blessing of abundance and family. But to be righteous meant especially that one cared for, or pleaded the cause of, the poor and the oppressed.

Such a concern is so thoroughgoing in the Old Testament that it is found in its every strata and expression: Law, Narrative, Poetry, Wisdom, Prophet.

Thus in the so-called Book of the Covenant (Exod 21–23), right in the midst of laws about seducing a virgin, sex with animals, practicing magic, and sacrificing to foreign gods, Israel is told not to mistreat or oppress an alien (22:21) and not to take advantage of a widow or an orphan (22:22). If they do the latter, they are warned, "My anger will be aroused, and I will kill you with the sword; your wives will become widows and your children fatherless" (22:23-24). In the same context they are commanded to lend to the poor without interest and to return a poor man's coat taken in pledge by sundown, because "I am compassionate." In Exodus 23:10-11, the Sabbath year was instituted expressly for the poor, as was the Jubilee year in Leviticus 25 and 27.

This same concern for the disenfranchised is thoroughgoing in Deuteronomy (e.g., 10:17-19; 15:1-4, 7-11; 24:14-22; 27:19) and in the Psalter, which especially extols God because he cares for the poor and comes to their rescue (e.g., 9:8-9, 12, 18; 10:9-14, 17-18; 12:5; 22:24-26; 35:10; 68:4-5, 10). In the great messianic Psalm 72, the "royal son," above all else, "will judge your afflicted ones with justice" (v. 2); "He will defend the afflicted among the people and save the children of the needy" (v. 4; see vv. 12-14).

Precisely because God *is* like this, and his Anointed One *will be* like this (see Isa 11:4; 42:1-4; 61:1), it is required of his people that they too plead the cause of the poor. This is especially true of those in authority. Thus it is only after he has murdered and stolen Naboth's vineyard that God's final judgment is pronounced on Ahab (2 Kings 21); and a strong part of Job's defense of his own righteousness was that he had in fact cared for the poor (29:11-17; 31:16-23).

All of this comes to its focal point in the prophets, whose condemnation of Israel repeatedly has three elements: idolatry, sexual immorality, and injustice to the poor (see Exod 22:21-27 above). It is because "they sell into slavery honest men who cannot pay their debts, poor men who cannot even repay the price of a pair of sandals" (Amos 2:6-7 GNB), and because they "twist justice and cheat people out of their rights" and "prevent the poor from getting justice in the courts" (5:7, 12) that God condemns Israel (see Isa 1:17, 23; 3:15; 5:8, 23; 58:1-12; Mic 2:1-2, 8-9; 3:1-4, 11; 6:8-12; Zech 7:8-14; and many, many others).

Righteousness in the Old Testament, therefore, calls for fair treatment of the poor. This is the way God is; this is the righteousness he demands. The poor are not to receive better things, or to be treated differently, but to be treated justly — and mercifully. Since the powerful and wealthy controlled the judges, the poor had only God to plead their cause. Thus it is not surprising that in messianic passages the needs of the poor are going to receive God's special attention.

It is within such a context of "fulfillment" that one must view the ministry of Jesus. But there is an added dimension. With him the Kingdom of God had made its appearance. This meant for him — and the early Christians — that in his own person and ministry the messianic age, the "blessedness" of the future, had dawned in human history. Jesus, therefore, is the beginning of the End, the inauguration of God's final rule. Thus he came with good news for the poor, which for Jesus meant not only the time of justice for the economically deprived, the vulnerable, but also the time of the gracious acceptance and forgiveness of sinners.

Precisely because with him the new age had dawned, this meant that the overthrow of the old order with its old values and injustices had begun. Because God's rule had come, people were freed from the tyranny of self-rule and the need "to get ahead." One cannot serve God and Mammon. Because God accepts and secures us, we need no longer be anxious about material things (Matt 6:24-34). And because God thus accepts and secures us, we can freely sell our possessions and give to the needy (Luke 12:32-34) and freely love our enemies and lend to them without expecting to get anything back (Luke 6:32-36). Indeed, the apostle John later says, if one has material possessions and cares nothing for the poor, such a person knows nothing of God's love (1 John 3:17-18; see 4:19-21).

It is within this twofold framework — the revelation of God as the one who brings justice to the poor and the inauguration of God's rule in the ministry of Jesus — that we must view the New Testament texts on money and possessions. Poverty *per se* is not being glorified, nor is wealth condemned. In the new age a whole new order has been inaugurated, with a new way of looking at things and a new value system.

It is clear that Jesus sees possessions in the old age as doing the possessing, not being possessed. Possessions tend to tyrannize or lead to a false security. Hence some of his strongest words move in this direction. "Woe to the rich, the full," he says (Luke 6:24-26), not because there is evil in wealth, but alas, because the rich "already have received their comfort." They see themselves as "in need of nothing," including God. Like the rich fool, they seek more and more because they think life consists in having a surplus of possessions. But they are "not rich toward God" (Luke 12:13-21).

"How hard it is for a rich man to enter the Kingdom," Jesus says. Indeed, it is easier for a camel to go through the eye of a needle. Jesus' point is that it takes a miracle for the rich to be saved, because they are secure in their possessions.

But it is equally clear that Jesus did not have an ascetic's eye toward property. If he had "no place to lay his head" (Luke 9:58), he and his disciples were in fact supported by the means of well-to-do women (Luke 8:2f.); and Peter owned a home in Capernaum to which Jesus repaired. In reflecting on the fourth commandment, he says that parents are to be supported from their children's possessions (Mark 7:9-13). In requiring money to be lent without hope of return there is the presupposition of money. Jesus went to dinners with the rich as well as the poor. Zacchaeus was not required to give up all his possessions: that he made a surplus reparation was the evidence of his salvation.

All of this is true because for Jesus wealth and possessions were a zero value. In the new age they simply do not count. The standard is sufficiency; and surplus is called into question. The one with two tunics should share with him who has none (Luke 3:11); "possessions" are to be sold and given to the poor (Luke 12:33). Indeed, in the new age *unshared wealth* is contrary to the Kingdom breaking in as good news to the poor. Thus, as Martin Hengel has so eloquently put it:

53

Jesus was not interested in any new theories about the rightness or wrongness of possessions in themselves, about the origin of property or its better distribution; rather he adopted the same scandalously free and untrammelled attitude to property as to the powers of the state, the alien Roman rule and its Jewish confederates. The imminence of the kingdom of God robs all these things of their power de facto, for in it "many that are first will be last, and the last first" (Mark 10:31; Matthew 19:30, 20:16; Luke 13:30). Of course, Jesus attacks mammon with the utmost severity where it has captured men's hearts, because this gives it demonic character by which it blinds men's eyes to God's will — in concrete terms, to their neighbour's needs. Mammon is worshipped wherever men long for riches, are tied to riches, keep on increasing their possessions and want to dominate as a result of them (*Property and Riches in the Early Church* [Fortress, 1974], p. 30).

It is precisely this new age attitude that one also finds reflected in the early chapters of the Acts. The early church was *not* communal. But it was the new community — the new people of God. Hence no one considered anything owned to be his or her own possession. The coming of the Spirit that marked the beginning of the new order had freed them from the need of possessing. Hence there was sufficiency, and no one was in need.

This same carefree attitude toward wealth and possessions also marks all of Paul. He is a free man in Christ, who knows contentment whatever the circumstances. He knows both want and plenty, both hunger and being well fed. He "can do all things" — which in this context clearly refers to being in need! — "through Christ who gives him strength" (Phil 4:10-13).

Thus he tells those who have nothing to be content with food and clothing: "People who *want to get rich* fall into temptation and a trap" (1 Tim 6:6-10). But then he remembers those who *happen to be rich*. They are to treat their wealth with indifference: they must not put any stock in it. Rather they are to be "generous and willing to share," for this is true wealth (6:17-19).

It seems to me that this is the biblical framework within which

American Christianity must once again begin to move and have its being. For many of us this will mean the adoption of a simpler way of life — not as Law, but as gratitude to Grace. For many it will also mean courage — courage to withstand the paganism of our materialistic culture and courage to give time and money to "unpopular causes," such as prison reform and world poverty. Such programs as Bread for the World, John Perkin's Voice of Calvary in Mississippi, the Catholic Worker Movement, and Charles Colson's Prison Fellowship are leading the way for us in these matters. God's call to us is for a return to biblical faith and to a radical obedience to our Lord Jesus Christ. This does not require poverty, but it does require righteousness, which in this context means to use our wealth not to manipulate others, but to alleviate the hurt and pain of the oppressed.

Chapter 6

Gender Issues: Reflections on the Perspective of the Apostle Paul

The task set out for me in this lecture is not an easy one, because so much of the controversy on gender issues in evangelical circles swirls around the Pauline data. Many of the problems, of course, are of our own making; here in particular examples of poor exegesis and selective hermeneutics are legion.[1] At issue as well is our tendency to throw too many disparate matters (male/female; husbands/wives; ministry/structures) into the same container and homogenize them.

But some of the problems clearly stem from Paul himself and the ad hoc nature of his letters. Lacking the need to systematize his own thinking, Paul spoke to different situations in different ways. Take for example his advice to widows in 1 Corinthians 7 and 1 Timothy

1. I do not mean to imply that I am free from such; but just a glance at the literature reveals how much of the exegesis is predicated on what a person was expecting to find before coming to the text.

The original "lecture" was not written out, but was given from notes. In this "written" edition, I have kept much of the flavor of the oral presentation (while removing many of the colloquialisms) and added a few notes for further reference.

5, where on the one hand (1 Cor 7:40) he discourages them to re-
marry, while on the other (1 Tim 5:14) he falls just short of com-
manding them to do so.[2] So at issue for us hermeneutically is how
to handle some of the differences that are actually present in Paul.

Perhaps the worst thing the evangelical tradition has done on
gender matters is to isolate them from the bigger picture of biblical
theology. Indeed, I think we are destined for continual trouble if we
do not start where Paul does: not with isolated statements addressed to contingent situations, but with Paul's theology of the
new creation, the coming of God's eschatological rule inaugurated by
Christ — especially through his death and resurrection — and the
gift of the Spirit.

PAUL AND THE NEW CREATION

Two texts in particular serve as the proper starting point here. First,
2 Corinthians 5:14-17, where Paul argues with the Corinthians who
are calling into question both his gospel of a crucified Messiah and
his cruciform apostleship. He responds that the new creation
brought about by Christ's death and resurrection nullifies one's
viewing anything any longer from the old age point of view (Gk. *kata
sarka,* "according to the flesh"). Christ's death means that the whole
human race has come under the sentence of death (v. 14), so that
those who do live (in God's new order) now live for the one who died
for them and was raised again (v. 15). The result, he goes on, is that
from this point on, to view either Christ or anyone/anything else
from a perspective that is "according to the flesh" is no longer valid
(v. 16). Why? Because being in Christ means that one belongs to the
new creation: the old has gone, the new has come (v. 17). It doesn't
take much reading of Paul to recognize that this radical, new order
point of view — life marked by the cross — lies at the heart of everything he thinks and does.

---

2. The NIV's "counsel" is much too soft here. The verb Paul uses, "I want" them
to, is precisely that used in 2:8 about men and women in prayer; and it is clear in
this passage that "want" has all the authority of apostolic command.

Which leads to our second text: Galatians 3:26-29. This passage offers the first of two conclusions[3] to the theological-scriptural argument of Galatians 2:16–4:7, in which Paul is adamant that Gentiles do not have to conform to the old covenant boundary markers/identity symbols, in order to belong to the new covenant people of God. The three primary markers were circumcision, food laws, and the keeping of special days. Although each of these is mentioned at some point in Galatians,[4] the major focus is on circumcision, because his opponents regularly appealed to it as the way Gentiles would also be included in the people of God (Gen 17:1-14).

To counter this argument and to recover his Gentile converts from further capitulation to the former covenant, Paul argues first from their experience of the Spirit (3:1-5), and then from Scripture regarding Christ (3:6-22). In his first conclusion Paul's concern is singular: that the old order has given way to the new — promised by God even before the covenant of circumcision. The old order, which helped to distinguish Israel from its Gentile neighbors, was signaled by the law — the legislation of the former covenant that, as Paul makes clear, was designed for sinners and assumed human fallenness. Paul's way of putting it in the present argument is that the law served to hem people in until the time for faith to come, with the appearance of God's Messiah (vv. 22-24). All of this because some Gentiles were being persuaded that to please God fully they had to adopt the identity markers of the former covenant as well.

"No," Paul says, as he now appeals to the new creation. Over against former slavery (Jews to the law; Gentiles to idols), he says emphatically: "In Christ Jesus, *all* of you are *children of God* [not

---

3. The second is 4:1-7, which picks up the themes of "sonship"/slavery under the imagery of the pedagogue from 3:24-25 (NIV "guardian," the educated slave to whom the children were entrusted for education) and of the life of the Spirit from 3:1-5, thus tying up the whole of the argument from 3:1.

4. An illustration over Peter's (not to mention Barnabas's) reneging on the Jerusalem agreement over keeping food laws (2:11-14) is what kicks off the rest of the argument of the letter; the matter of "days" is denounced in 4:8-10 as a reversion to slavery. The same three "boundary markers/identity symbols" make up the argument of Romans as well. Circumcision is argued against in ch. 4, while days and food laws come under scrutiny in 14:1–15:4.

slaves] through faith" (v. 26), which is further evidenced by their "one baptism" (v. 27). All who have been baptized into Christ have thereby been clothed with Christ. Behind this sentence lies the baptismal theology of Romans 6, full of "new creation" eschatological presuppositions. Death and resurrection have taken place in Christ. As believers go through the waters of baptism, we assume our own role in that death and resurrection, thus dying to the old and rising into newness of life — into the new creation.

In verse 28 Paul comes to the conclusion that we have been led to expect, namely, that in the new creation there is neither Jew nor Greek. But right at that point, typically of Paul, he recognizes that the new creation obliterates *all* the old sociological categories that separated people. So he adds, what is true of Jew and Greek is equally true of "slave and free, male and female." His point: In our baptism "into Christ" and through the work of the Spirit we enter the new order, the new creation; and where death and resurrection have taken place, the old distinctions have been obliterated.[5]

Paul, of course, does not mean that the three categories themselves cease to exist in the new creation, at least not in its present "already/not yet" expression. To the contrary, as part of the continuity between the old and the new, all of us are some combination of the three: e.g., Gentile, free, female. What has been obliterated is the *significance* of these distinctions and the (basically divisive) *values* — ethnic-racial (Jew/Gentile), socioeconomic (slave/free), and sexual-gender (male/female) — based on them.

Our difficulty with understanding the truly radical nature of

---

5. It has often been argued against this point of view that this is a soteriological text, having to do with people from all of these categories coming to Christ on the equal ground of faith. So it is, but to divorce soteriology from ecclesiology in Paul is theologically disastrous. Salvation in Paul's view has not to do with God's populating heaven with countless individuals, but with creating a people for his name through Christ and the Spirit. It is in the creation of a people for his name that one finds the continuity with the former covenant. Thus, the present text is ecclesiological by the very fact that it is soteriological. The certain evidence for this is the companion passage to this one, 1 Cor 12:13, which is expressed in soteriological categories but is ecclesiological to its core. See G. D. Fee, *God's Empowering Presence* (Peabody, MA: Hendrickson, 1994), pp. 178-82.

Paul's assertion is twofold. First, most contemporary Christians have very little sense of the fundamental eschatological framework which was common to the entire New Testament experience, and which in fact was the *only* way the earliest believers understood their existence. Second, Western culture in particular is quite foreign to that of these early believers at some fundamental points. In the culture into which Paul is speaking, position and status prevailed in every way, so that one's existence was totally identified with and circumscribed by these realities. By the very nature of things, position and status gave advantage to some over others; and in Greco-Roman culture, by and large, there was very little chance of changing status.

Thus Gentiles had all the advantages over Jews, so Jews took refuge in their relationship with God, which they believed advantaged them before God over the Gentiles. The hatreds were deep and mutual. Likewise, masters and slaves were consigned to roles where all the advantages went to masters;[6] and the same was true for men and women, where women were dominated by men and basically consigned to childbearing. In fact, according to Diogenes Laertius, Socrates used to say every day: "There were three blessings for which he was grateful to Fortune: first, that I was born a human being, and not one of the brutes; next that I was born a man and not a woman; thirdly, a Greek and not a barbarian."[7] The Jewish version of this, obviously influenced by the Greco-Roman worldview, is the rabbi who says that "everyday you should say, 'Blessed are you, O God, ..., that I'm not a brute creature, nor a Gentile, nor a woman.'"[8]

It is especially difficult for most of us to imagine the effect of Paul's words in a culture where position and status preserved order through basically uncrossable boundaries. Paul asserts that when people come into the fellowship of Christ Jesus, significance is no

6. This is one place, it should be pointed out, where change could take place in that culture, because slavery was not based on race as it was in the tragic history of the United States. Rather, it was based primarily on war, captivity, and economics, so that people could change status; e.g., in economically hard times people could sell themselves into slavery, and masters often manumitted slaves.

7. 1.33 (Loeb Classical Library).

8. Talmudic tractate *Menahoth* 43b (Epstein translation).

longer to be found in being Jew or Greek, slave or free, male or female. The all-embracing nature of this affirmation, its counter-cultural significance, the fact that it equally *disadvantages* all by equally *advantaging* all — these stab at the very heart of a culture sustained by people maintaining the right position and status. But in Christ Jesus, the One whose death and resurrection inaugurated the new creation, all things have become new; the new era has dawned.

The new creation, therefore, must be our starting point regarding gender issues, because this is theologically where Paul lived. Everything else he says comes out of this worldview of what has happened in the coming of Christ in the Spirit.

THE IMPACT

What, then, was the impact of this radical worldview on male/female relationships? We begin by noting that in the new creation both of the essential matters from the first creation — mutuality/complementarity and differentiation — are restored. It is the new *creation*, after all. This can best be seen in two passages in 1 Corinthians — 7:1-40 and 11:2-16 — where some women (apparently) in the believing community have overdrawn the implications of their new eschatological existence.[9] That is, they appear to have been arguing for, or assuming, a "mutuality" without "complementarity," as well as for the elimination of differentiation. This Paul simply will not allow since these, too, are a part of the creation, both old and new.

What most likely lies behind this is their view of speaking in

9. This view stems from several realities in the letter, especially the fact that directly following a passage where Paul forbids the men to go to the prostitutes (6:12-20), he takes up the issue of some who are rejecting sex within marriage, on the grounds that "it is good for a man not to touch a woman." When he comes to the issue of divorce (v. 10) — the logical corollary of their position — he does the most non-cultural thing: he argues that a woman should not separate from her husband, and then, almost as an afterthought, says that the same holds true for husbands as well, of course. For the full argument supporting this view, see G. D. Fee, *Commentary on the First Epistle to the Corinthians* (NICNT; Grand Rapids: Eerdmans, 1987), pp. 10-13, 267-70.

tongues. In 13:1 Paul says, "If I speak in the tongues of men and of angels." This may have been a reference to the Book of Job, where Job's daughters are given a waistband to put on, by means of which they are transported into heaven by the Spirit, and by the Spirit speak the dialect of the angels. This appears to have been a common understanding, that the one speaking in tongues was speaking the language of heaven.

A kind of ultimate "spirituality" seems thus to have set in at Corinth, which included a disregard for the body. Very early on Christians got messed up about the body's being a good thing (given that God created it). Such a view goes back at least to Paul's Corinth. Because they were already speaking the language of the angels, some of the women considered themselves already as the angels (who neither marry nor give in marriage, Luke 20:34-36) and thus were arguing for no sex in marriage (7:1-16) and were also removing a symbol of differentiation (11:2-16).

Paul corrects the former abuse by insisting that each person's body does not belong to oneself, but to the other (7:3-4) — not in an abusive, possessive way, of course, but as gift to the other person. Because of mutuality and complementarity in the marriage relationship, every husband and every wife must be in continuing sexual relations with each other (v. 2) and must stop defrauding one another on this matter (7:5). Thus this passage radically alters the sexual relationship within marriage. Instead of the more common pattern of sex as something the husband does to his wife for his sexual gratification, sexual intimacy is a celebration of belonging to one another, where one's "body" is not one's own private possession; rather, both partners give their bodies for the other in a relationship of mutual love.

In the same way Paul argues in 11:2-16 that wives continue to wear the head-covering because it served as a symbol of differentiation between men and women. Although it is often suggested otherwise,[10] this passage has nothing to do with the subordination of

10. Based primarily on a reading of v. 3 that suggests that "head" equals to be "over the other" in some way. But this sentence is created by Paul as a kind of word play on the word "head," based on the problem lying literally on the wife's head, so

women to men — a view arrived at by making verse 10 say the opposite of what Paul in fact asserts. The Greek text cannot be more
clear, that a woman has authority over her own head "because of the
angels."[11] If there is still plenty of obscurity about the latter phrase
(I think it relates to their being like the angels), there is no question
about who has authority over what. The woman in Christ has authority over her own head, even with regard to the traditional head-
covering. But Paul wants her to use that authority to maintain differentiation in the new order. That the issue has to do with differentiation between male and female is found in the rhetoric of verses 5
and 6. If she insists on removing the familiar sign of differentiation,
Paul argues, why not go the whole way of "shame" (to herself in this
case) and have her head shaved or shorn — in that culture evidence
of the "male" partner in a lesbian relationship.[12]

---

that he can establish a point of reference for the issue of shame. The meaning of
"head" is much debated, of course, but the so-called "Greek" view, which seems to
make the most sense of all the data in the passage, is expressed in the interpretation
of Cyril of Alexandria (*Arcad.* 5.6): "Thus we say that 'the head of every man is
Christ.' For he was made by him . . . as God; 'but the head of every woman is the
man,' because she was taken out of his flesh. . . . Likewise 'the head of Christ is
God,' because he is of him by nature."

11. For the evidence of this see Fee, *First Corinthians,* p. 519. There is no known
instance in the language where the combination of subject the verb "have," the object "authority," and the preposition "over" are passive with regard to the subject,
i.e., in which the subject is under someone else's authority, rather than exercising
authority over the object of the preposition. There is not a reason in the world to
think it is otherwise here, especially so, when Paul immediately qualifies the
woman's authority over her own head (with regard to wearing or not wearing the
head covering) by insisting that "in the Lord, however, woman is not independent
of man, nor man of woman" (v. 11).

12. For the evidence see Fee, *First Corinthians,* pp. 510-12. It has often been as-
serted that the shaved head was a sign of prostitution in Corinth; but there is not a
known piece of evidence for such in the literature of antiquity. For Paul same-sex
intercourse is a matter of denying the differentiation and mutuality of creation,
which is what lies behind Paul's strong denunciation of homosexuality in Romans
1:24-27. Those who have exchanged the truth about God and have believed the lie,
Paul says, have expressed their denial of the truth of creation, what God has done,
by same-sex intercourse. And God has given them over because they have refused to
believe the truth about God. This, of course, sounds like a very harsh word to peo-

The bottom line issue in this text has to do with "shame" (see vv. 4, 5, 6, 13, 14) in a culture much like present-day Asian cultures, where shame counted for everything. With a wonderful word play on "head" — where the issue literally lay — Paul argues that the wife was shaming her husband (her "head" from v. 3) by removing the symbol of differentiation, just as a husband would have shamed Christ by wearing the wife's symbol.

In response Paul does not subordinate the woman, but rather insists that she maintain this symbol of their differences. In a purely *ad hoc* way, Paul argues in verses 7-9 that a wife should not shame the one whose glory she is by creation. To be sure, that is often read as referring to subordination. But nowhere else does "glory" appear in Scripture as having to do with subordination. The woman, rather, is seen as complementary, the glory of the man, as is evidenced in the narrative of Genesis: she was made from man and for man (vv. 8-9), not to be subordinate to him, but as his glory, to complement him. That she has regained her place of mutuality lost in the Fall is made clear in verses 10 to 12. Immediately following verses 8 and 9, he concludes by first stating the reality of the woman's own authority over her (now literal) head: "For this reason, the woman has authority over her own head because of the angels." "Nonetheless," he qualifies in verse 11, with both 8 and 9 and now 10 in view, the wife is not to exercise her "authority" as one who is independent of her husband; nor are they to understand verses 8 and 9 wrongly: because "in the Lord" there is total mutuality. After all, God has ultimately reversed things — man now comes from the woman — so that "in the Lord" neither is independent of the other, because "everything comes from God."

Thus, the thrust of this argument is twofold: that the woman should continue with the cultural symbol of differentiation because of the issue of shame — but that this should not be understood to

---

ple who are oriented toward same-sex relationships, but the fact is, "male and female, God created them"; and Paul sees very clearly that the obliteration of that created expression is in fact an elimination not only of what God has created but what is also being restored in the new creation. Why else, one wonders, would he single out these two relationships — men with men and women with women? Notice also the language of shame that is persistent in that text.

mean subordination, but mutual interdependence in the Lord. The new creation has not removed mutuality and differentiation, but has restored it. In the Lord male and female are both one and different. Thus men and women equally pray and prophesy, the two basic forms of worship in the Christian assembly (which took place in homes), but do so as male and female, not as androgynous beings.

THE IMPLICATIONS FOR SOCIAL STRUCTURES

Given Paul's basic theological stance, and its impact on male/female (especially husband/wife) relationships, the question that remains for us is the problematic one: What are the implications of all this for social structures? To get at this issue we need to return to the three sets of structures singled out in Galatians 3:28, that "there is neither Jew nor Greek, slave nor free, male nor female." It is clear from several passages in Paul that he is not arguing that the new creation eliminates the fallen structures in which some of the differences exist. What Paul does with those structures is to radicalize them by putting them into the context of the cross. Everything is moderated by the fact that the cross rules over all.

Take slavery as an example. On the one hand, in Colossians 3:22–4:1 and Ephesians 6:5-9 Paul calls on both masters and slaves to live as brothers and sisters in Christ, without urging that the structure itself be eliminated. On the other hand, in Philemon he radicalizes the relationship in such a way that it no longer carries significance. Paul does not say, "Philemon, stop having slaves"; what he says is that now "you have Onesimus back for good — no longer as a slave, but better than a slave, as a beloved brother" (vv. 15-16). How, one wonders, can the old structures carry their former significance in this context — where the slave who has stolen and run away, and who in Roman law merited death, is now accepted back as a dearly loved brother in Christ? And remember that both the letter to the Colossians and to Philemon were read publicly in the gathered community, where both Philemon and Onesimus were present together to hear what God had established through the cross. The old distinctions may still exist in a sociological way, to be sure, but they cease to have meaning when both master and slave own the same master, Jesus Christ.[13]

When we turn to male and female relationships (in a culture where this primarily had to do with wife and husband in the home), we find the same thing. The problem for us in reading the texts (especially the "house codes" in Colossians 3:18–4:1 and Ephesians 5:18–6:9) is that we have scarcely an inkling as to how much Paul was in fact radicalizing the Greco-Roman home. Thus before looking at the Ephesians text, one needs to have a sense for the sociology assumed by the passage. And here architecture says a great deal. Although the early believers lived in other kinds of settings — tenements; shopkeepers, who lived above their shops; etc. — this passage assumes a larger household of a kind shown in figure 1 (on p. 67),[14] which included wives, children, and slaves.

The basic sociological model for this kind of household is that of patronage, meaning a communal relationship between unequals. In this kind of relationship each of the unequals benefits the other. The master of the house benefits the rest of the people in the household by providing for them; they benefit him by doing his bidding (slaves, in particular). The wife would benefit by the fact that she could now exist in a home besides that of her father, and of course the householder benefited because hopefully she would bear him male heirs.[15]

13. This truth should have brought all the nonsense in North American Protestant arguments in favor of slavery over the past three hundred years to its knees in absolute repentance. What has gone on in my own country (the United States) on this matter is sheer craziness, since Philemon is the clear evidence that "brother in Christ" means that black and white *must* eat together at the same table; the table of the Lord, eaten in the context of a meal, is the great equalizer. Otherwise the gospel of our Lord is betrayed at its core.

14. For this diagram and much of the description that follows I am indebted to Carolyn Osiek and David L. Balch, *Families in the New Testament World, Households and House Churches* (Louisville: Westminster/John Knox Press), p. 8 and throughout.

15. In the Greco-Roman world, girl babies were very often "exposed," put in the dump and left to die. It is the males who count because they carry on the family line. Enough females were obviously kept for the purposes of the male, but a female baby was absolutely chattel and was at the total discretion of the father whether he wanted to keep it or not — and I mean the father, not the parents.

Figure 1:
A typical *domus*

Key:
1. fauces
2. shop
3. atrium
4. impluvium
5. cubiculum
6. tablinum
7. andron
8. peristyle
9. triclinum
10. oecus

(Drawing by Deborah Wells)

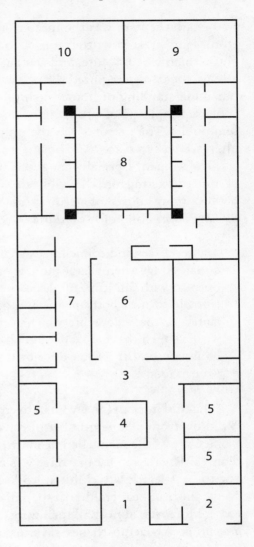

By law, the man was the master of his household (thus the patron). Paul's text is written into a context of "totalitarian patriarchy," which was absolute, and sustained by law.[16] Usually, but not always, the patron required the household to serve his gods. Unlike our understanding of home, such a household was not a place of consumption, but of production; not a private refuge, but often semipublic. The patron's was the only public role, and the atrium often served as a place to do business and was basically open to others. The women, especially daughters, lived in the rear and were not permitted to stray into the public domain of the house — for fear of her becoming abused or a seductress. Much of this is described in a passage from Philo of Alexandria:

> Market-places and council-halls and law-courts and gatherings and meetings where a large number of people are assembled, and open-air with full scope for discussion and action — all these are suitable to men both in war and peace. The women are best suited to the indoor life which never strays from the house, within which the middle door is taken by the maidens as their boundary, and the outer door by those who have reached full womanhood.[17]

What did it mean for a woman to enter such a household as wife? We know from a large number of census lists from Egypt that the average age of the man when he married was 30, of the woman, less than 18. The reason for marriage was not "love" in our usual sense, but to bear legitimate children, to keep the family line going; indeed, failure to bear children, especially sons, was often cause for divorce. Moreover, almost all men were (from our point of view) promiscuous. As Demosthenes says in an offhanded, matter-of-fact

16. We need also to appreciate, of course, that in all such situations where the law allows the most despicable kind of behavior, there are always people who function as beneficent dictators; and we know of many of these from Greco-Roman culture. My concern is not to paint the picture as utterly bleak, but to point out that a thoroughly totalitarian patriarchy was simply assumed under the law itself.

17. Philo, *The Special Laws* 3.169 (trans. by F. H. Colson in the Loeb Classical Library, 7.581).

way: "Mistresses we keep for the sake of pleasure, concubines for the daily care of the body, but wives to bear us legitimate children."[18] Wives, therefore, were often promiscuous as well — although they tried to be more discreet, since their infidelity was a matter of shame!

The idea that men and women might be equal partners in marriage simply did not exist, evidence for which can be seen in meals, which in all cultures serve as the great equalizer. In the Greek world, women scarcely ever joined their husbands and his friends at meals; and if they did, they did not recline at table (only the courtesans did that), but sat on benches at the end. And they were expected to leave after eating, when the conversation took a more public turn. It is especially difficult for most of us even to imagine our way back into such a culture, let alone to have any sense of feeling for it. Which is what makes what Paul actually says so counter-cultural in every way, without eliminating the structures themselves.

Our difficulty in getting back into Paul's text is that we are heirs of a culture in which two major events in the past three hundred years have radically altered Western culture forever, and turned the basically patronal culture that preceded it completely on its head: the so-called Enlightenment and the Industrial Revolution. The Enlightenment, with its emphasis on the individual, created a culture in which individual rights came to be regarded as the highest good, so much so that by the late twentieth century the concept of individual rights has finally superseded that of the common good (an idea with a rich history that has now become passé).

But the Enlightenment alone did not create the structural changes in our understanding of home and family (after all, look at the British manor house, with its "enlightened" autocrat, that has got such bad press in a whole series of recent movies). It took the Industrial Revolution to turn things around; and it did so by drawing both men and women out of the home into the marketplace, so that, whereas in 1885 in the United States 88 percent of all goods were produced in the home, by 1915 that was totally reversed.

With these, and all the more so if we add the onset of the "tech-

18. *Oration* 59.122.

nological age," also came the wonderful opportunities that women now enjoy: equal opportunities for education, including finally the right to vote and to serve in almost every way in the public domain. But it also resulted in our homes being thought of as havens for rest and, until recently, as the place for the nuclear family to exist — a concept almost foreign to Paul's world.

But the Apostle Paul preceded these events by two thousand years, with the message of a crucified Messiah, which was culturally subversive at its core. Indeed, perhaps the most radical thing was that all people who participated in God's new creation also shared a common meal together and thus celebrated their Lord's death until he was to come again — which, as 1 Corinthians 11:17-34 makes clear, created considerable tension for the traditional household.

When we turn at last to Ephesians 5, we need to begin where Paul's own sentence begins, with verse 18, because "be [keep] filled with the Spirit" is the only imperative in the passage until verse 25 ("Husbands, love your wives"). Thus Paul is urging that believers be filled with the Spirit, and evidence that by singing, giving thanks, and submitting to one another.

In the relationships that follow, three things need to be noted. First, in the ordinary household the husband, father, and master are all the same person, while the wife, children, and slaves were different persons. Second, when Paul tells the wives to submit, and children and slaves to obey, he is not offering some new idea, or countering insubordination, he is merely speaking within the culture. But those who are filled with the Spirit and worship Christ as Lord, do so as those serving their true Lord, not an earthly one.

Third — and here is the truly radical moment — both the structure of the passage and the word count (four words to the husband for every one word to the wife) indicate that the emphasis lies with the householder, the husband/master/father. And the only thing Paul says to him is repeated three times: "Love your wife." Love *(agape)* is what rules, and *agape,* it must be noted emphatically, does not refer either to romance or sex. Rather, it refers to his giving his life in loving service to her for her sake.

One should note especially the regular emphasis on loving his *own wife.* That eliminates the courtesans. Love your wives (v. 25);

love your own wives (v. 28); love your own wives (v. 33). She is the one who deserves all of your love and commitment of loving service. The model, as throughout the New Testament, is Christ's love for the church which is expressed in his death on the cross. The imagery Paul uses is that of a man taking a bride, deliberately echoing language from Ezekiel 16, where God betroths the naked and orphaned teenager and washes her and dresses her in the finest of clothes. Paul now images the husband as treating his wife as just such a bride, adorned and glorious to behold.

It is assumed in this text, of course, that the husband will continue to provide leadership in the household. But such leadership will be radically transformed into caring for the people, not having them around to serve his own self-interests. And that is why Paul goes on to speak of the slaves and the children. In each case, the husband, the master, and the father is the person Paul is after. If he can radicalize the home in light of the cross, the life of the child, of the slave, and of the woman is set into new perspective in the new creation.

So where does that put us hermeneutically? I would argue that the structures are ultimately quite immaterial for believers; that is, first-century households can no more serve as models for Christian homes at the turn of the twenty-first century, than the Roman Empire with its self-serving, destructive economic policies and its insistence on emperor worship, should serve for contemporary political structures. All structures, ours as well as theirs, are predicated altogether on cultural givens. There simply is no biblical structure for the household.

Thus in our culture, structures tend to depend largely on the two people involved with regard to their own giftings, personalities, and how they relate to each other. But whatever the structure, at issue is that we live Christ-like in our relationships with one another in our homes. God calls us to *shalom*, to be filled with the Spirit, thus submitting ourselves to one another in reverence to Christ, to love with Christ's love by self-sacrificial giving of ourselves. And I would suggest that if we do that well, the matter of structures will pale into insignificance.

WHAT ABOUT MINISTRY?

The Pauline texts show a rather consistent view with regard to "ministry," meaning serving the church and the world in a variety of ways. Everyone, man and woman alike, minister within the context of their own gifting by the Holy Spirit. At the crucial point of ministering by verbal gifting, Paul consistently says such things as "all may prophesy" (1 Cor 14:23), to which 1 Corinthians 11:2-16 bears corroborating evidence. Despite some voices to the contrary, Paul made no distinction between men and women in the use of any verbal gifting (prophecy, tongues, teaching, revelation, etc.). Gifting by the Holy Spirit was the only criterion, and the Holy Spirit was obviously gender-blind, since he gifted men and women at will.

When we move to the question of "offices" in the church, of course, we move into an arena where Paul supplies us with almost no evidence. The idea that there are some who serve as "priests," and that they should be males (thus keeping alive the strictures of the older covenant!), would be about as foreign to Paul as one could get. In any case, it seems clear that "function" preceded the concept of "position." That is, people functioned as prophets or teachers before they were called that; there were not preordained "offices" that they should step into.

Thus the ultimate question before us in the matter of "gender and ministry" is not whether women ministered — of course they did — but whether, given the cultural norm, they also stepped into roles of leadership (which in itself is a nebulous term in light of the Pauline evidence). That they did so in fact would be consistent with the radically counter-cultural sociology that found expression in the believing community, as outlined above.

Thus, one of the more remarkable moments in Paul's letters (but seldom thought so by us, because we tend to read our culture back into the text) is his greeting at the end of Romans to Priscilla and Aquila (16:3-5). That he mentions Priscilla first, that he praises them because "they [plural] risked their lives for me," and that he greets the church that meets in *their,* not Aquila's, house, is sure evidence that something has already been transformed by the gospel.

This is also the significance of such passages as Colossians 4:15

("Nympha and the church that meets in *her* house") and Acts 16:13-15, 40 (where the first believers in Philippi met at Lydia's house). When a church met in this kind of household, where they would gather in the atrium, the semipublic area where business was regularly carried on, the householder would naturally serve as the leader of the house church. That is, by the very sociology of things, it would never have occurred to them that a person from outside the household would come in and lead what was understood as simply an extension of the household. To put it plainly, the church is not likely to gather in a person's house unless the householder also functioned as its natural leader. Thus Lydia would have held the same role in the church in her house as she did as master of the household.

Other passages reflect the same reality, beginning with the evidence from Philippians 4:2-3. Euodia and Syntyche must have had ministry in the church because of the language Paul uses. They labored side by side with Paul in the gospel, as did the rest of his fellow workers, meaning the others who ministered in the church besides Euodia and Syntyche. Given this language, had these been men, everyone to a person would grant that they were leaders in the church in Philippi; and even now the only ones who think otherwise, think so simply because Euodia and Syntyche were women. Paul's language is decisive here: they were leaders in the church in Philippi.

The well-known sociology of Macedonia[19] corroborates this as well. Despite what was said above about women in public life, Macedonia was well-known as an exception to the norm; from way back women held significant positions in public life. It is therefore not surprising that evidence of their leadership in the church turns up in Philippi.

Similarly, in Romans 16:1-2, Phoebe is the *diakonos* of the church in Cenchrea, meaning she is the servant of the church. This is the same language Paul uses elsewhere of himself and others, in terms of their giving leadership to the church. In this case he adds that she

---

19. For this matter see W. W. Tarn, *Hellenistic Civilization* (Cleveland: World Publishing Co., 1952), pp. 98-99.

has also been a *prostatis* to many people, including Paul. There is plenty of good evidence that this word in this case probably means that she has served as the "benefactor" of the church and of others as well.

Finally, in Romans 16:7 Paul singles out Andronicus and Junia, probably husband and wife, who were apostles before Paul himself. Despite attempts on the part of some to turn Junia into a man (only because she is here called "an apostle"), that simply will not do. No such name as Junias is known to exist in the Roman world. She and her husband together served as apostles, pure and simple, although the term in this case, as it almost surely does in 1 Corinthians 12:27 as well, refers to a "function," not an "office."

The only exception to this consistent picture is the *ad hoc*, very case-specific instruction Paul gives in 1 Timothy 2:11-12. And this is clearly the "odd text out," not the norm. In the context of 1 Timothy, the issue is not church order but false teaching. It is equally clear from the evidence of Acts 20 and from the evidence of 1 and 2 Timothy, that the false teachers are local elders who are going astray after false teaching. That is why Paul has such a problem in this letter, and why Timothy is in for such difficulty, because as a younger man he has to stop — even to excommunicate — the elders who are involved in the false teaching. The evidence of 1 and 2 Timothy together makes it further clear, that these straying elders have found fruitful ministry in the households of some younger widows. In 2 Timothy 3:8 in particular, they are said to have wormed their way into the homes of these women, weak-willed and silly women Paul calls them, who are always trying to learn but never able to come to a knowledge of the truth.

In 1 Timothy 5:13 Paul had earlier said of these younger widows, that they go about from house to house being *phluaroi*, which despite our English translations to the contrary, does not — in fact cannot — mean "gossips," but "speakers of foolishness." This word is used in all kinds of philosophical texts of people who "prate foolishness," meaning, of course, who teach a philosophy different from the author. Thus these younger widows were going around from house to house passing on the foolishness of the false teachings. Paul's admonition to them is singular: Because they have already gone astray after Satan (5:15), they are to marry (v. 14; over against his advice in 1 Cor 7:39-40), to manage their households well (assume the woman's role in a married household), and "to bear children."

This last piece of advice picks up from the companion passage in 2:11-15,[20] where this is precisely how "they will be saved." Thus in this singular place in the New Testament, these widows, who are in process of repeating Eve's transgression through Satan's deception,[21] are forbidden to teach or domineer. Rather, they are to get married and bear children?

Finally, I would like to remind those who think that this text controls all the others in the New Testament, that if one thinks verse 11 is a verse for all times and all circumstances, then why not verses 9 and 10 that precede it, and verse 15 that follows it, that says that women will be saved by bearing children?

Paul of course surely does not intend that these younger widows will be given eternal salvation by bearing children. This is simply a synecdoche; "bearing children" is one activity (to be elaborated in 5:14) that represents his greater concerns. They are to be "saved" in this case by no longer adhering to, and spreading, the false teaching. This is why he gives his later directive for them to get married, because by getting married they come back into a situation where they will not be spreading false teaching and thus fall prey (as Eve did before them) to Satan's deceptions. What he does later in chapter 5, of course, is to have Timothy excommunicate the elders who are responsible for all this, thus indicating that the two groups in chapter 5 (widows and elders) are the ones causing the trouble for the church.

The point in all of this is that this one text,[22] which has clear

---

20. The only two uses of the *teknogonein* (to bear children) word group in the New Testament occur in these two verses (2:15 and 5:14).

21. Although Paul says that "Adam was created first, then Eve" in v. 13, his point is not that this makes only men qualify as teachers, but that the one who was created second was first in transgression. And it is not her teaching that he takes up, but her "salvation."

22. On the inauthenticity of 1 Corinthians 14:34-35, see Fee, *God's Empowering Presence*, pp. 272-81.

case-specific reasons for existing, should not be used to set aside the rest of the evidence. If we do not have more such evidence, we must remember that these texts were written in the first century, into a context like that described above. The wonder is that we have as many such texts as we do. What is significant about them is that the texts that do exist are not trying to "teach" or "correct," they are simply stating what was in place, all of which was the result of the new creation.

CONCLUSION

The net result of all this seems clear enough: that Paul does not tear down existing structures, but neither does he sanctify them. Everything for him begins with Christ, his death and resurrection, whereby he established the new order, the new creation. In the new creation, two things happen: the relationship between man and woman in the first creation is restored, but that relationship must be lived out under the paradigm of the cross. In Christ Jesus there is neither male nor female, not meaning that differentiation has ceased, but that both alike enter the new creation on the same footing, and thus serve one another and the rest of the church in the same way their Lord did — by giving themselves to the other(s) out of love. Ministry is thus the result of God's gifting and has nothing to do with being male or female, any more than it has to do with being Jew or Gentile, or slave or free.

Chapter 7

The Bishop and the Bible

On the basis of John Spong's statements published in the preceding issue of *Crux,* one could cavalierly note that a response to his use of Scripture would have to be included among the legendary collection of the "world's smallest books." For in fact there is very little that passes as biblical interpretation in his presentation; what appears instead are several moments of rhetorical, out-of-hand dismissal of the biblical perspective on homosexuality, set up by a railing against those who "use the Bible to perpetuate the attitudes and prejudices of the past" (p. 21). Nonetheless, one must also take seriously the bishop's own profession of love for the Bible, and his desire to "rescue it for the church from the clutches of fundamentalism." What I propose to do in this response, therefore, is to take both the bishop and Scripture seriously, and to do so (1) by suggesting that in the final analysis his statements about love for Scripture and his cavalier attitude toward it in the debate are quite incompatible, and (2) by offering an interpretation of the Pauline texts on the issue of homosexuality that is at once faithful to the point of view of Scripture and compassionate to those in the gay community, as compassion is defined by the gospel.

1. If one cuts through the rhetoric so that one can see what the bishop is trying to do, two things emerge. First, although I was not able to hear the debate personally, even a casual reading of Spong's

prepared address, as well as his off-the-cuff remarks, makes it clear that he was playing to his audience. The problem with such a method is that it may very well backfire on a speaker, in two ways: On the one hand, while such a play to the audience may win points with the already-converted, it is highly unlikely that it will be persuasive to those whose minds are not yet made up and would like to hear careful, reasoned arguments. Unfortunately, for those whose minds are also already made up on the other side, such argumentation has the effect of belittling, and therefore of being anything but Christlike. On the other hand, it leaves the bishop highly suspect as to whether he had carefully thought through the matter of audience at all. If his goal was to caricature those who disagree with him, so that those who agree might have reason to thumb their noses at other believers, then he surely succeeded. If it was to win over unbelievers for the Christian faith, Spong's presentation, which tends to belittle the Bible in the process, hardly approaches genuine evangelism.

From my point of view, such rhetoric functions as a totally "lose-lose" proposition: (a) it divides Christians in the public forum, rather than demonstrating that Christians can disagree in public without resorting to worldly methods of trying to conquer opponents; (b) it may indeed offer solace to fellow travelers on the issue of homosexuality, but it scarcely offers them a positive attitude toward Scripture, so that the net result will finally be an inability to hear the gospel itself, since that rests on Scripture alone and nothing else. To put all of this another way, the problem with Spong's attack, despite his protests to the contrary, is that it can only have the effect of demeaning Scripture, both in the eyes of those whose love for the Bible is equal to (in light of Spong's rhetoric I would think "greater than") that of Spong himself, and in the eyes of those who do not know our Lord Jesus Christ and whose only hope of hearing the gospel lies in the very Scriptures that Spong belittles before their eyes.

Second, in playing to his audience in this way, Spong thereby also tries, on the one hand, to distance himself as much as possible from a view of Scripture that he calls fundamentalistic, and, on the other hand, to approach the issue of homosexuality by way of an argument from cultural relativity that rather totally removes any moral implications from such behavior.

Spong's opposition to fundamentalism is thoroughgoing, but not always fair, mostly because he seems determined to throw the net too widely, so that the term includes people like Stott, whose own work and attitudes are as far removed from the fundamentalism that Spong eschews as is Spong himself. But "fundamentalism," it should be noted, may refer either to a set of conclusions about Scripture that are often unduly "literalistic" and, from my point of view, obscurantist, or to the mindset of those who hold such views. One of the primary characteristics of this mindset is the tendency to divide the whole world into two camps: "us" and "them."

Unfortunately, this is the very mindset that Spong himself adopts, both in his present address and in most of his earlier books. His rhetoric has the clear effect of placing all people in two camps regarding Scripture — especially on the matter of homosexual behavior — Spong's and everyone else's, the latter whom, besides "fundamentalist," he brands variously as "naive," "sexist," and "blatant homophobics," who "quote the Bible with abandon in order to uphold their perspective." That, of course, is precisely the attitude that he himself caricatures at the beginning as "fundamentalistic."

The bishop is right; fundamentalism should be rejected, but fundamentalism of all kinds, including that which he both rails against and models, where those who disagree with his own passionately held positions are dismissed by name-calling rather than by taking their contrary positions seriously as carefully and prayerfully considered. The problem with Spong's view of Scripture is not simply that it represents "unreconstructed liberalism,"[1] but that by its narrowing of the perspective so starkly, Spong himself seems unaware of the large "middling" group, both evangelical and otherwise, who probably represent the majority of contemporary New Testament scholars. I do not herewith suggest that the majority has it right, heaven forbid, but that one represents a kind of scholarly naiveté that does not take that

1. A liberalism, it should be noted, that most biblical scholars have assumed to have been brought to an end through the rise of neo-orthodoxy and existentialism, which themselves are now passé within the academy.

majority with some considerable seriousness when doing biblical studies. And this Spong seems incapable of doing.

One of the fundamental postulates of hermeneutics is that interpreters come to texts laden with presuppositions, both about the texts they are interpreting and the world in which they live, including their own baggage. I do not herewith consider myself exempt from such; indeed it is always easier to see this baggage in another than in oneself. But surely the bishop's strong reaction to his own personal history colors his thinking and negates his ability to take Stott's arguments seriously in their own right. My own experience with scores of students over many years who have made a journey similar to Spong's, usually to a lesser degree, is that they "love" people only in the direction they are traveling, but cannot find the grace to do so in the direction from which they have come. Despite his protestations of holding in "honor" the church of his youth, the rhetoric of his prepared address speaks a different story of prejudice and unresolved anger.

2. As to his use of Scripture, several things may be said, carefully, I hope, since not everything that one believes can emerge in the format in which this "debate" was carried out. Not having heard the debate, I read his *Rescuing the Bible from Fundamentalism* (San Francisco: Harper, 1991), so that I might be a bit better informed about his way of reading and understanding Scripture. To his discredit, the method revealed there represents the same kind of rhetoric and the same failure to take seriously New Testament scholarship as a whole as one finds in the present debate. Whatever else, exegesis is not John Spong's strong suit. In some ways I knew that beforehand, since my previous knowledge of his work was through his "historical reconstruction" of Jesus which argues that Jesus was the groom at the wedding of Cana with Mary Magdalene as his bride. This has rightly been dubbed "silly" by a knowledgeable lay theologian, because it deals with "history" in such a non-historical, purely speculative way, yet wants to be taken seriously by others. As one may well expect, no New Testament scholar gives such a view the time of day. Exegesis and history must be made of sterner stuff![2]

2. In this regard, cf. the critique of his most recent Jesus book (*Born of a Woman:*

The most obvious rhetorical ploy in Spong's argumentation in the debate with Stott is to be found in the fact that his longest and most impassioned attack is not over the issue of homosexuality at all but against Scripture's alleged patriarchalism. The stratagem seems plain enough: to attack Scripture's (consistent) attitude toward homosexuality as obscurantist by attacking its (from Spong's point of view, equally obscurantist) attitude toward male-female relationships. But "guilt by association" will not do.

To be sure, on the matter of homosexuality as behavior Scripture has a universal point of view: that such behavior lies outside the intent of creation and is consistently labeled as sinful. The texts which speak to this issue are thus consistent with the overall view of Scripture at every significant point of Christian theology: creation, the fall, redemption, and consummation. Those who take Scripture's own view on this matter are not therefore merely "applying ancient biblical verses"(!) to this issue. We are trying, on the contrary, to be sensitive to the whole of Scripture and its view of what God is doing in our world through Christ and the Spirit.

On the other hand, on the matter of male-female relationships the Bible is not consistently patriarchal, at least not as it is defined in Spong's prejudicial way. While no one will deny that the Old Testament presupposes a patriarchal worldview, as do all of its neighboring cultures, it neither defends nor theologizes that presupposition. That is simply the "stuff" of the world into which Israel was brought into existence. But the perspective of the New Testament is strikingly different. While the world into which the gospel came, both the Jewish and Greco-Roman world, one needs to point out was still patriarchal, both Jesus and Paul offer a radically altered perspective, in which they not only affirm women but see the good news of the gospel as destroying any significance attached to racial, social, and sexual distinctions, which belong to human fallenness. After all, it is the Paul whom Bishop Spong appears to dislike so in-

---

A Bishop Rethinks the Birth of Jesus, 1992) by N. Thomas Wright (*Who Was Jesus?* [Grand Rapids: Eerdmans, 1992]), who deals with Spong about as kindly as a New Testament scholar can, but who also exposes the various idiosyncrasies of Spong's kind of "exegesis."

tensely who said that "there is neither Jew nor Greek, slave nor free, male nor female, for you are all one in Christ Jesus" (Gal 3:28).[3] That the Bible has been used by some of its well-meaning friends to continue to attach significance to these distinctions does not make the Bible itself homophobic, nor those who stand against Spong on the matter of homosexual practice.

What is striking in Spong's presentation is his apparent need to use this form of guilt by association as his way of categorically dismissing those who hold a different view of Scripture from his, since he seems to have much more difficulty dealing with the biblical texts on both of these issues. What he is tacitly arguing, of course, is that patriarchalism and opposition to homosexuality are at root the same thing. But this is not the perspective of the Bible, nor, others of us would argue, should they ever be so easily confused. A lack of compassion by those who hold such views is correctly fought against; but Scripture makes sharp distinctions between morality and mores, even if Spong would have us believe that the distinction is wrong. I, too, condemn in the name of the God who has revealed himself in Christ all forms of racism and male domination of women. And I was doing the latter long before it became a fad on the part of the religious establishment of which the bishop is representative. It ought to be condemned because it is wrong; and it is wrong not because I or Spong pronounce it so, but because Scripture has revealed it so as over against all that redemption in Christ means and provides "for us people and our salvation."

3. What is easily the most incongruous aspect of Spong's view of

---

3. It is this same Paul, one should also note, who plays the lie to several of Spong's (unsupported and unsupportable) assertions, as e.g., "in the Scriptures, divorce was permissible, but only for the male" (p. 26). This is partial truth at its worst and has the effect of dismissing Paul from Scripture. Anyone who has worked carefully through 1 Corinthians 7 (esp. vv. 10-11, 12-16) will recognize not only that women could divorce their husbands, but also that the whole chapter, with its consistently balanced clauses between men and women, demonstrates that Paul is not the male chauvinist that Spong makes him out to be. Indeed, when Paul says that "husbands do not have authority over their own bodies but that their wives do" (1 Cor 7:2-4), he has gone miles beyond most cultures, including most people in Spong's own modern culture.

Scripture, is his professed love for the Bible, on the one hand, and his thoroughly cavalier attitude toward it, on the other. He offers us a clearcut choice: His view or Scripture's own perspective. Scripture is variously set aside for modernity; indeed "a Bible that reflects tribal, racial, nationalistic, and sexual prejudices needs to be confronted" (p. 22). I would agree; but the larger question is whether Spong's is an adequate view of the Bible as a whole, or whether he is jousting still with the windmills of his past, especially with the way his fundamentalistic tradition interpreted the biblical text. Spong's basic hermeneutical stance on these matters is to distinguish between "the letter of Scripture" and "the spirit of Scripture" a common, but exegetically indefensible, use of a Pauline text to support a modern idea. What is at stake is not the "letter" or "spirit" of texts, but the intent of any and all texts within the larger context of a given writer and finally of the whole of Scripture itself.

It should be noted at this point that most of Spong's execration of biblical texts (on pp. 22-23) reflects either especially poor exegesis on his part (including 1 Cor 11:7-12 [he reads vv. 8-9 exactly backwards and acts as if Paul did not also write vv. 11-12, which were offered apparently as correctives precisely so that one would not read vv. 7-9 the way Spong does]; 1 Tim 2:9-15; Rom 1:26-27) or positions espoused in some texts that do not themselves reflect the view of Scripture as a whole. Whatever else one may wish to say of Spong's rhetoric, this is simply bad form as far as interpretation is concerned.

Here we are clearly dealing with basic issues as to the nature of Scripture: what it means for Scripture to be the Word of God, and how it functions as such in the life of the believing church and of the believer. And here Spong and I part company rather radically. He sees views like mine as anachronistic at best, as spiteful at worst; I see his as sitting in judgment on the biblical text in such a way that the living God has very little chance of sitting in judgment on him and calling his own sins into account.[4] When one can so easily pick

---

4. On these matters see esp. "Issues in Evangelical Hermeneutics: Hermeneutics and the Nature of Scripture," *Crux* 26 (1990): 21-26 (repr. in *Gospel and Spirit, Issues in New Testament Hermeneutics* [Peabody, MA: Hendrickson, 1991], pp. 24-36). Sev-

THE TEXT AND THE LIFE IN THE SPIRIT

and choose where and how he will allow God to speak to him or her through Scripture, especially on what Scripture considers matters of righteousness, why should one want to have Scripture at all?

In the final analysis, Spong pushes us to make a clearcut choice between him, with his obvious enchantment with modernity, and Paul, who says that when he proclaims Christ he speaks the very message of God. Faced with such a choice, and it is the only choice Spong allows us, I will go with Paul every time. For in Paul I find the love of God and God's wrath against our sin brought together in the cross; in Spong I find merely "soft mush," in which the only "biblical" defense of homosexuality is a paragraph which does not have a single moment of Scripture in it, where gay and lesbian people are "demanding" to be seen as "holy," created thus in "God's image," and "called to the fullness of their gay and lesbian humanity in God's Holy Spirit." The bishop may indeed believe that to be so; but he certainly cannot sustain that view on the basis of the church's Scriptures, either from specific texts or from its overall perspective. And for me to speak so is not to speak as homophobic, but is to speak the truth in love on the basis of what one finds in the biblical texts themselves. In answer to Spong's rhetoric, "Why is it that some of us think today that people who wrote the Bible between 1000 B.C. and 150 A.D. knew enough about homosexuality to pronounce judgment on it for all time?" the obvious answer is, "because, as the church's basic creeds have always maintained, we believe that Scripture is inspired by the Holy Spirit, and that what God himself has inspired is a word for all seasons." If Paul is homophobic, then Scripture itself is homophobic. And if I must choose between Spong and the Bible, then I must go with the Bible, which is not homophobic, but is God's Word of redemption and transformation to all who will hear and obey.

4. That leads, finally, to some words about the Pauline texts that Spong dismisses out of hand. Regarding Paul's views of homosexual practice as the ultimate expression of God's having given people up

eral matters addressed in the present essay have been previously spoken to in this former one, especially the matter of distinguishing "evangelical" from "fundamentalist" and "liberal" hermeneutics, and how each of them works in practice.

to their own degradation, Spong responds, "What a strange idea! And it's not the only time that Paul is wrong." There you have it; modernity, clothed in a bishop's robe and wearing a mitre, over against the apostle himself, without whom there would have been no Christianity within which Spong could be bishop. But Spong's interpretation[5] of Romans 1 misses Paul exegetically by a mile, and theologically as well.

At issue in Romans 1 is human fallenness, described by the apostle as "the godlessness and wickedness of people who suppress the truth of God by their wickedness." The ultimate form of such wickedness, Paul says, based on the futility of thinking about life apart from God and without thanksgiving to him, is idolatry, in which mere creatures "exchange the glory of God" for the exaltation of the creature. They simply "believe a lie," both about God and about themselves. The ultimate expression of this exchange, Paul concludes, is homosexual activity, in which those created in God's image as male and female so as to reproduce the race — procreation, not recreation, is after all the primary reason for sexuality — exchange their natural, created sexuality for that which is not natural, precisely because it cannot lead to the reproduction of more human beings equally created in God's own image. Persistence in such activity is condemned along with all other forms of idolatry, in which the creature and his or her desires is preferred to the Creator; and this is the consistent view of Scripture.[6] This does not make homosexual practice any worse than the other sins enumerated in vv. 28-30; but neither does it allow that such "unnatural" activity is less than what it is: a form of choosing the creature over against the Creator, just as is adultery and promiscuity.

---

5. Spong asserts (quite incorrectly) that "Paul actually asserts that passions of a person toward one of his or her own sex is in fact punishment from God on those who do not worship properly." When Paul says that "God gave them up," that may be a form of judgment to be sure, but it is not so much a form of "punishment" from Paul's perspective as it is an expression of the lengths to which the "creature" will go in his or her struggle against the Creator, who has made people sexual beings, male and female, precisely so that they might procreate the race.

6. On this matter, and the other Pauline texts as well, see now D. F. Wright, "Homosexuality," in *Dictionary of Paul and His Letters* (Downers Grove: InterVarsity, 1993), pp. 413-15.

But in any case, judgment is never the final word; it is merely the first word. The final word is redemption. And those who are involved in homosexual behavior are invited to this redemption along with those of us whose idolatries have taken different forms. Thus, in the vice list in 1 Corinthians 6:9-11 Paul includes two words for practising homosexuality[7] along with eight other expressions of "wickedness" that if persisted in will exclude people from the final eschatological kingdom. But the last word is the word of redemption: "But such were some of you; but you were washed, you were sanctified, you were justified by the authority of Jesus' name and by the power of the Spirit."

And here is where Spong's and an evangelical understanding of Christian faith part company radically. Spong persists in a brand that is thoroughly unbiblical at its crucial center; "redemption" for him means passive tolerance on the part of God toward human fallenness, in which God in Christ affirms us in our fallenness, forgives us for it, but leaves us there. And because in our fallenness that seems so decent of God, we would like to think that such decency is what redemptive love is all about. But that is precisely the "soft mush" of traditional liberalism.

The New Testament has a different point of view, in which God's love is both stronger and gentler than that promoted by the bishop. In love Christ has not only redeemed us, and thereby delivered us from our rebellion against him, but has given us his Holy Spirit, his own empowering presence, so as to transform us, recreate us if you will, back into his likeness. Redemption in Christ and by the Spirit, therefore, does not whitewash sinners and leave them in their sins, but transforms sinners, recreating them in God's own likeness, to reflect his image and glory which we in our fallenness here so thoroughly debased. Such transformation may not "cure" our orientation toward sin; but the Spirit, Paul says, and thousands have experienced it so, is sufficient. Those who walk by the Spirit are

---

7. Attempts to water down these words, such as one finds in John Boswell and others, is so much special pleading. Besides my commentary on this passage, see esp. D. F. Wright, "Homosexuals or Prostitutes? The Meaning of *Arsenokoitai* (1 Cor 6:9; 1 Tim 1:10)," *Vigiliae Christianae* 38 (1984): 125-53.

promised that they will not fulfill the desires of the flesh, including the desires that have to do with our modernity, in which we try to outsmart God as to what "good" means for our fallen human race. In this matter, and obviously in others as well, give me the word of the living God, and deliver me from the words of a bishop who has given up Scripture for his own modernity.

THE TEXT AND THE LIFE
OF THE CHURCH

Chapter 8

The Holy Spirit and Worship
in the Pauline Churches

Let me begin by defining the term "worship," since it is another of those "accordion" words that tends to gain meaning by however much air one pumps in or out of it. Strictly speaking, worship has to do with homage or adoration offered to God, which is what is intended by the Greek word most often rendered into English as "worship." In English, however, the word "worship" came to pick up an extended meaning, not found in Greek, having to do with what takes place when Christians gather for that purpose. Usually it refers to the whole event, sometimes as an adjective (e.g., "worship service") but often simply as a noun (e.g., during "worship"). A more recent nuance of this latter usage narrows its point of reference to one or more of the activities directed specifically toward God, especially singing, plus the praise and prayer that occur during singing (e.g., "our worship time").

My interest for this lecture is with the so-called "worship service," for which, it must be pointed out, there is no word in Paul's Greek. When he does refer to this event, he uses either of two verbs that mean "to assemble" or "to gather together." Thus he refers to the Corinthians as "assembling as a church" (1 Cor 11:18; lit. "when you gather together in assembly"), or of "the whole church assembling/gathering in the same place" (14:23).

My interest here is in exploring, first, the *nature* of these "gather-ings" in the Pauline churches, and, second, in *the role of the Spirit* in their gatherings.

We should note at the outset that this is a somewhat tenuous task, in that Paul offers no specific instruction on such matters in his let-ters. Which makes perfectly good sense, since "worship" is something they simply did, very much like eating, so that there was no reason for instruction or analysis. What we learn, therefore, comes to us by way of Paul's correcting some abuses. And since these are so case-specific, we must admit that we know far less than we should like to know, and of course far less than we would like to admit to.

What I propose to do is quite simple. First, I will offer a very brief overview of what is available to us as working data; second, I want to make some observations about several aspects of these data, trying to ferret out what we can learn about worship in Paul's churches; third, I note the crucial role of the Spirit in their worship; and fi-nally, I conclude by focusing on a single aspect of worship, namely the role of singing.

I. THE DATA

Although our data from Paul regarding the church gathered for the worship of God are relatively sparse, there is just enough for us to make some general observations — and we must be especially careful in this case not to make too much of his silence regarding certain matters.

We begin by noting that the language of "gathering" for the pur-pose of worship in the sense we have defined it occurs only three times in the Pauline letters, all in 1 Corinthians, and always in the context of correcting an abuse. First, in 11:17-34, it occurs in a con-text where Paul is admonishing the "haves" as to how they are treat-ing the "have nots" (the language of v. 22) at the Lord's Table. Here the language of "gathering" occurs five times (vv. 17, 18, 20, 33, and 34); in v. 33 Paul specifies, "when you gather *to eat*," referring of course to the eating of the Lord's Supper that has been the point of contention in what has preceded.

Second, the terminology also occurs in chapter 14 (vv. 23 and 26), where Paul is correcting the Corinthians' singular enthusiasm for speaking in tongues in the assembly. One should also note v. 19 where he says that "in the assembly I would rather speak five intelligible words than thousands of unintelligible ones" and v. 33 where he refers to what takes place "in all the churches of the saints," referring specifically to their gatherings.

The third occurrence of this language is in the very difficult sentence in 5:3-5, where in the context of excommunicating the brother living in incest, Paul says (literally), "when you and my spirit assemble together with the power of the Lord Jesus." What this means specifically is a matter of some debate, as you might well understand, but there can be little question that Paul is referring to the gathering of the whole church. Most likely Paul understands himself to be present by means of the Holy Spirit, as his letter, which he understands to function as a prophetic word in their midst (14:37), is being read in the assembly.

It is probably of some importance to note that in two of these instances (11:20 and 14:23) Paul speaks of their "gathering together in the same place," while in 14:23 he also notes that it is the "whole church" that is gathering in this way. Furthermore, in 14:26 Paul actually specifies some of the activities that take place when the church is thus gathered: "When you assemble," he says, "each one of you has a psalm, a teaching, a revelation, a tongue, an interpretation." I tend to think that we should probably add "and so forth" to this list, since Paul proceeds in what follows to take up not only tongues and interpretation, but also "prophecy and discerning prophecies," neither of which is mentioned in v. 26 (although it is possible that "revelation" stands for prophecy in this case).

Although these are the only places where this specific language occurs, there are at least five other passages which also reflect Christian worship, and perhaps several others as well.

a. Paul refers to the Lord's Table in two other places in 1 Corinthians. In 10:16-22 he argues that the Corinthians' own meal in honor of the Lord means that they cannot join their neighbors in the meals at the pagan temples, since that means to eat in fellowship with demons.

93

b. In a much more allusive way, in 10:1-4 Paul images Israel in the desert as having had their own form of baptism and Lord's Supper. Of the latter he says, "they all ate the same spiritual food and drank the same spiritual drink," referring to manna and the water from the rock.

c. In 1 Cor 11:4-5 Paul refers first to men and then to women as "praying and prophesying." Although this passage does not mention the assembly as such, both the language and its location in the letter argue for a church context. In the immediately following passage where he corrects their abuse of the Lord's Supper, Paul begins in v. 17 by stating, "in the following instructions I do not commend you, for when you assemble it is not for the better but for the worse." This would seem to imply that what has preceded also took place in their assembling together.

d. Finally, in the twin passages in Col 3:16 and Eph 5:18-20 Paul speaks of their being filled with the Spirit, so as to teach and admonish one another with songs of various kinds, as they offer praise and thanksgiving to God. What makes it clear that this is referring to Christian worship is not only the mention of teaching and singing, but that in Col 3:16 he specifically mentions the "message about Christ" as dwelling in their midst as they teach and admonish one another through singing.

Along with these rather clear allusions to Christian worship, we could add some more indirect references, especially those passages that refer to the "church that meets in [their/her] house" (Rom 16:5; 1 Cor 16:19; Col 4:15), as well as those passages that state or imply that Paul expected his letters to be read in the gatherings of God's people: for example, Col 4:16 (where the Colossian and Laodicean letters are to be exchanged and read in the churches), plus the doxology at the end of Philippians and the grace that concludes all of his letters, both of which function best in the context of worship.

II. WHAT WE CAN LEARN FROM THE DATA

When we turn next to an analysis of these data, we must begin by noting how little we really learn about many things that interest us.

94

For example, we learn nothing at all about such matters as *time, frequency, size, order, or leadership*. The references to the churches of various households indicate that the Greek word *ekklesia* has just enough flexibility to it, so that although in places it can refer only to the people themselves, at times it likewise refers to the gathered assembly of the people, as it does always in the Greek Old Testament. But we are quite in the dark about these gatherings. Even the language in 1 Corinthians 14:23 referring to the "whole church" assembling is ambiguous, whether that means the whole of a given house church or the whole of the believers in Corinth — presumably from several house churches — assembling in a larger place of some kind. If it refers to given house churches, then each gathering is relatively small by our standards, since archaeology has yet to discover a villa in Corinth that could house more than 50 people comfortably in the atrium. If it refers to all the house churches meeting together, the question remains as to where and how.

In terms of *participation* we learn that men and women participated equally, since this is said specifically in 1 Corinthians 11:4-5 and implied in the repeated "all speak in tongues" in 14:22-23 and "all may prophesy one by one" in v. 29. Furthermore, there appears to have been a great deal of Spirit-led spontaneity on the part of the whole community. This is certainly implied in the description in 14:26, and made certain by the description of prophecy and discernment in vv. 29-32 with the admonition that the "S/spirits of the prophets are subject to the prophets."

While we might guess that there were one or several giving *leadership* to this spontaneity, we don't have a clue as to who or what form this may have taken. Paul's emphasis is on the (at least potential) participation of the whole body. What this also means, to anticipate the next section, is that the role of the Spirit, who gifted women and men alike to speak to the community, makes it especially tenuous for us to look to the Jewish synagogue for help in these matters. Not only did they worship in anticipation of the coming Spirit, and therefore without him, but also there was no place or any kind for women to participate.

What we are left with, therefore, are references to various "activities," for want of a better term, which cover a broad range — from the eating of the Lord's Table together, to singing, to various forms of speech (prayer, prophecy and discerning prophecies, tongues and interpretation, and teaching, including the reading of Paul's letters). But there is just enough ambiguity in each of these areas to cause us to be especially cautious about our own pronouncements.

Most difficult for us to know is (1) whether these various references give us all we need to know about their worship, and (2) whether the two very different kinds of activity involved in eating the Lord's Supper and in speaking and singing occurred at the same gatherings, or in gatherings of two different kinds. In light of the passing reference to "praying and prophesying" in 1 Cor 11:4-5, followed immediately by the correction of the Lord's Table, which are held together by the twin introductions in vv. 2 and 17, I am inclined to think that these two (prophesying and the Table) occurred at the same gatherings; but such inclination falls far short of certainty.[1]

What does seem clear from these various references is that the "activities" of worship were double directional — toward God, on the one hand, and toward the community, on the other. This is almost certainly how we are to understand the reference to "praying and prophesying" in 1 Corinthians 11:4-5, where prayer represents speech that is directed toward God and prophecy represents speech directed toward the community. Similarly, the singing in Colossians 3:16 and Ephesians 5:18-20 involves "teaching and admonishing one another" while also "offering thanksgiving to God." Likewise, the fellowship at the Lord's Meal, according to 1 Corinthians 10:16-22, involves participation in the Lord and participation in the body of Christ, which Paul interprets as the church.

What all of this seems to indicate, therefore, is that worship in the Pauline churches was much more varied, with a much greater combination of spontaneity and set activities than most of us know in the later church. The singing, which included "psalms, hymns, and Spirit songs," probably refers to the singing of both spontane-

---

1. Such a view is supported in part, at least, by the Jewish philosopher Philo of Alexandria's description of the Jewish adaptation of the Greek symposium, where a meal was followed by discourse and singing (see *On the Contemplative Life,* 70-72).

ous songs under Spirit inspiration by an individual ("each one of you has a psalm") as well as to songs previously composed and sung by the whole. The speaking included prayer directed toward God, including tongues and their interpretation which in the public assembly Paul understands to be praise or thanksgiving directed toward God and interpreted for the people. It also included all kinds of speech directed toward the people, including inspired utterances such as prophecy or revelation, or a message of wisdom or knowledge, or spontaneous teaching, as well as the reading of Paul's letters, which would also imply the reading of the Old Testament Scriptures.

It is very likely, we should add finally, given that the context of all of 1 Corinthians 12 and 14 is the community at worship, that the gatherings of the people in the presence of the Spirit also included in an ongoing way a variety of non-verbal supernatural phenomena such as healings, miracles, and moments of special faith. This is made certain not only by how Paul sets forth the Spirit manifestations in 12:7-11 (where each one is given a manifestation for the common good) but also by the fact that in Gal 3:5 Paul specifically says that in supplying the Galatian believers with the Spirit in an ongoing way, God performs miracles among them. This does not imply that "worship" was the only context for such Spirit activity, but that it certainly served as one significant context for such.

When we add all these observations together, we must admit that we don't really know very much, but we know just enough to be intrigued to the full. Wouldn't one love to be the proverbial fly on the wall in the gathering of God's people in one of the early Gentile churches under Paul's jurisdiction? My guess is that most of us would not be quite sure where we were, since the Lord's Table took place in the context of a meal together and the worship included so much Spirit-led spontaneity. I have often wondered, if the roles could be reversed (i.e., if Paul could be the proverbial fly on the wall in one of *our* gatherings, either of the more liturgical variety or more Baptist/Presbyterian variety), whether Paul would recognize himself as in a Christian gathering for the worship of God. But I refuse to do more than wonder, because we simply do not know enough.

But that does leads me, then, to the matter of the role of the Holy

Spirit in all of these activities, which is probably the factor that separates us more than any other from worship in the Pauline churches.

III. THE ROLE OF THE SPIRIT

What is most notable in all the available evidence for worship in the Pauline churches is the common denominator of the presence and power of the Holy Spirit. This, of course, is abundantly clear in the long discussion in 1 Corinthians 12–14, where Paul variously refers to any and all of the various activities mentioned as "given by the Holy Spirit." The one and the same Spirit, Paul says, disperses all of these as he wills (12:11); the person speaking in tongues utters mysteries by the Spirit, he adds (14:2); I will pray and sing with my S/ spirit, he goes on (14:14-16), meaning that the Holy Spirit by means of tongues speaks praise and thanksgiving to God through Paul's own spirit.

This latter passage probably offers us the clue to the unusual expressions in 1 Corinthians 5:3-5. Despite most English translations to the contrary, Paul does not say, "as though I were present," meaning because I am not there in body I am not really present. Rather he says clearly that he is *in fact* present when they gather. His way of expressing this is "my Spirit is present." Since in 14:37 he makes it clear that he understands what he writes to them in this letter to function as a Spirit-inspired prophetic word, most likely he envisions himself as present by the Holy Spirit when his letter is being read in their midst.

It seems certain, therefore, that the various spontaneous activities mentioned in 14:26, "where each one of you has something to contribute for the edification of the body," are clearly to be understood as inspired by the Spirit. The whole of this argument means that the "teaching" envisioned in 14:6 and 14:26 is not a sermon or lesson prepared beforehand, but is given spontaneously by inspiration of the Spirit. Although one cannot be certain, it is possible that Paul thus understood *prophecy* as being a *revelation* of some kind, very likely of the kind mentioned in Galatians 2:2 which prompted Paul to go up to Jerusalem and consult with the leaders there.

Teaching, on the other hand, according to Colossians 3:16 has the "message about Christ" as its primary content, implying that the teaching that comes by way of letter, song, or inspired utterance focuses on the gospel — and its ramifications (after all, they both teach *and admonish* one another).

More difficult to assess is the role of the Spirit at the Lord's Table. We need to begin by noting that the word "Spiritual" in Pauline usage refers not to something "mystical" or "religious" or "internal," with reference to the human spirit, but rather refers primarily (if not altogether) to the Holy Spirit. Therefore, we must surely understand Israel's analogy to our Lord's Supper, with its "Spiritual food and Spiritual drink" to be an allusion to Paul's understanding of the Spirit as present when believers eat the bread and drink the wine of their Supper.

How the Spirit was present is more difficult to assess. It is altogether unlikely that Paul understood him somehow to invade the bread and wine itself. More likely he understands the Spirit's role to be present to create and empower the two-way *koinonia* (participation/fellowship) between believers and their Lord and with one another as they eat the bread and drink the wine. After all, in Paul's view the Spirit is responsible for the creation of the church as Christ's body, represented in our "Spiritual food," and is the agent of the New Covenant represented in our "Spiritual drink."

The key to all of this, of course, is Paul's larger understanding of the Spirit as the renewal of God's Presence both within and among his people. For Paul the resurrection of Christ and the gift of the Spirit meant that the final, messianic age had already dawned. The Spirit for him was both the evidence of the presence of the future and the guarantee of its final consummation. The coming of the Spirit meant that the New Covenant promises of Jeremiah and Ezekiel, where God would put his Spirit within his people's hearts and they would both live and obey him, had been fulfilled. Likewise, the coming of the Spirit meant that Joel's prophecy had been fulfilled, so that all of God's people — old and young, men and women, slave and free — would function as prophets.

The key to their worship is thus to be found in passages like 1 Corinthians 3:16-17, where Paul urges that they recognize what it is they are destroying with their merely human wisdom and division, namely, God's temple in Corinth — the church itself. Do you not know who you are, he asks? You are God's temple in Corinth, the place where the eternal and living God has chosen to dwell in your city. And you are that precisely because the Spirit of God dwells in and among you. Thus, when the church assembles, Paul argues later, Paul himself is also present by the Spirit as is the power of the Lord Jesus, also by the Spirit.

It is no wonder, therefore, that Paul sees all that takes place in such a gathering to be the working of the Holy Spirit.

IV. WORSHIP AND THE TRINITY

That leads me finally to take a closer look at the twin passages in Colossians 3:16 and Ephesians 5:18-20. My interest in doing so is twofold: (a) to note the role of singing in the worship of the Pauline churches; and (b) to note that truly Christian worship is ultimately Trinitarian.

Colossians 3:16 appears toward the conclusion of a series of exhortations (vv. 12-17) that indicate what it means for the believers in Colosse to live as those "raised with Christ" (v. 1), while Ephesians 5:18-20 occurs as the transitional word between the long list of general exhortations that began in 4:17 and the more specific ones that deal with relationships within the Christian household.

Here are passages full of intriguing information about worship in the Pauline churches. I begin by noting what we learn from *the opening exhortations* ("let the word of Christ dwell in your midst richly" and "but be filled with the Spirit").

1. Everything about the contexts, and the language of both sentences in particular, indicate that Paul is here reflecting on the Christian community. These are not words for the individual believer, but for believers as the people of God in relationship with one another. In Colossians that is especially clear. Beginning with v. 12, everything has the community in sight, since everything is for, or in light of, "one another." Thus in the immediately preceding exhortation (v. 15), which sets the pattern for the present one, they are to let

the peace of Christ rule in their hearts, since it is to this that they have been called together as one body.

Verse 16 views these relationships within the context of the gathered people of God at worship, where they are to teach and admonish *one another* as one way that the word of Christ will dwell "in them" richly. This means that the prepositional phrase "in/among you," even though it modifies the verb "indwell" and would ordinarily mean "within you," here means "in your midst." The indwelling "word of Christ," therefore, in its two forms of "teaching and admonishing one another" and of "singing to God," has to do with the church at worship.

If the community context in Ephesians is less immediately certain, it is clearly in view, since the whole passage from 4:1 through chapter 6 takes up community life, how they are to "maintain the unity of the Spirit in the bond of peace" (4:3).

2. In the same vein, it is significant to note that the compound participles, "teaching and admonishing," are the same two that Paul used in Colossians 1:28 to describe his own ministry. Here, then, is clear evidence that Paul did not consider "ministry" to be the special province of either apostles or office-holders. As in the earliest of his letters (1 Thess 5:14), these kinds of activities in the Christian assembly are the responsibility of all believers.

This is quite in keeping with the picture that emerges in 1 Corinthians 14:26 as well, where he admonishes in a presuppositional way, that "when you come together, *each one* has a hymn, etc. . . . for the strengthening of the church."

3. The primary concern of the exhortation in the Colossians passage is with the "word of Christ." In Paul this invariably means "the message of the gospel with its central focus on Christ." This, after all, is what the letter is all about: Christ the embodiment of God, Christ the All-sufficient one, Christ, creator and redeemer. Paul now urges that this "word of Christ," which in part he has already articulated in 1:15-23, "dwell in their midst" in an abundant way.

In so doing, they will reflect precisely what we learned about worship from 1 Corinthians 11:4-5. Part of their activity will be directed toward one another ("teaching and admonishing one another"), and part toward God ("singing to God with your hearts").

Thus the "riches" of the gospel are to be present among them with great "richness." The structure of the sentence as a whole indicates that songs of all kinds are to play a significant role in that richness.

4. The parallel passage in Ephesians makes explicit what we would have guessed in any case, that Paul considers all of this activity to be the result of their being filled with the Spirit. Thus, however we are to understand the adjective "Spiritual" in relation to the various expressions of song, Spirit songs are at least one expression of the Spirit's presence, whose "fullness" will guide and inspire all of the worship in its several expressions.

When we turn from these opening clauses to the rest of the two sentences, we learn still more about Paul's understanding of Spirit-inspired worship.

1. It needs to be noted, first of all, that where the Spirit of God is, there is also singing. The early church was characterized by its singing; so also in every generation where there is renewal by the Spirit a new hymnody breaks forth. If most such songs do not have staying power, some of them do, and become the treasure trove of our ongoing teaching and admonishing of one another, as well as of our constantly turning to God the Father and God the Son and offering praise by inspiration of the Holy Spirit.

2. But having said that, it is doubtful whether we are finally able to draw fine lines between the three words used to describe the singing. The "psalm," for example, may well include the Old Testament Psalter, now taken over into the worship of the Christian communities; but one would be bold indeed to limit it to such. This, after all, is the word used for the (apparently) more spontaneous singing of 1 Corinthians 14:26, and its corresponding verb is likewise used in 1 Corinthians 14:15 to refer to Spirit-inspired "praise to God" in tongues, as well as with the mind. Thus, even though New Testament usage is undoubtedly conditioned by the fact that the hymns of Israel were called "psalms," there is no good reason to understand it as limited to those hymns. What is suggested by this word, of course, is a song that is in praise of God.

So also the word "hymn." In the Greek world, this word was used exclusively of songs sung to deities or heroes, and thus would never be used, for example, of the bawdy songs of the bistro. Therefore, "hymns" also refer to singing praise to/about God, or in the case of the New Testament to/about Christ as well, as the evidence from the Revelation makes especially clear.

The third word, "songs," covers the whole range of singing, so Paul qualifies it here with reference to the Spirit. As already noted, the adjective *pneumatikos* ("spiritual") in Paul ordinarily refers to the Spirit, either directly or indirectly. Here in particular the ordinary meaning prevails. We are dealing with songs that are inspired by the Spirit. This is most likely an indication of a kind of "charismatic hymnody," similar to that alluded to in 1 Corinthians 14:15-16 and 26, in which Spirit-inspired, and therefore often spontaneous, songs were offered in the context of congregational worship.

Therefore, even though "Spiritual" could well modify all three nouns — the psalms and hymns would also be "of the Spirit" — it is more likely that it is intended to modify "songs" only, referring especially to this one kind of Spirit-inspired singing. The word "songs," after all, is the one which the recipients of the letter would least likely associate with worship, since it covers the whole range of "songs" in the Greek world, whereas the other two are usually sung to a deity.

3. Very likely we have fragments of such psalms, hymns, and Spirit songs embedded in our New Testament documents. The Revelation, for example, is full of "new songs" sung to God and to the Lamb. That is almost certainly the case with Ephesians 5:14 and 1 Timothy 3:16 as well. But more significantly for this letter, the considered opinion of most New Testament scholars is that Colossians 1:15-18 also reflects such a hymn about Christ. If this is so, and there are no good reasons to doubt it, then that would also explain why Paul thinks of these various kinds of hymns and Spirit songs as a means of their "teaching and admonishing one another." Such songs are at the same time creedal, full of theological grist, and give evidence of what the early Christians most truly believed about God and his Christ.

4. The background to such two-dimensional worship, hymns that are at once directed toward God and a means of teaching and admonishing one another, is to be found in the Old Testament Psalter. There we find dozens of examples of hymns addressed to God in

the second person, which also have sections in the third person, extolling the greatness or faithfulness of God for the sake of those singing to him.[2]

The use of hymns in the New Testament documents indicates how clearly they also function in this two-dimensional way for the early church. Most of them are about Christ, and as such are both in worship of him and for the continuing instruction of God's people. The clear implication of 1 Corinthians 14:15-16 and 26 is that "Spirit songs" in the Pauline communities are also to be understood in this way. Singing "with the mind" (= singing intelligible words by the Spirit) is understood as praise to God, and something to which the rest respond with the Amen; and the "psalm" in 14:26 is precisely for the "building up" of the others. Unfortunately, many contemporary Christians do not think of their singing in these terms, and thus miss out on one of the significant dimensions of our reason for singing.

5. Let me conclude, finally, by noting that in its own non-reflective way, Colossians 3:16 is a crucial "Trinitarian" text. There are more than a score of such texts in Paul. But in contrast to the others, where the Father initiates salvation, which the Son effects and the Spirit applies, here the order is reversed. Christ still plays the central role, hence they must let the "word of Christ" dwell lavishly in their midst. But the same Spirit who applied salvation now helps to initiate response through Spirit-inspired songs reflecting the message about Christ, and all to the praise of God.

The God who created and redeemed is worthy of all praise. The Spirit who was present at creation and became present to bring us to life in redemption, now leads us in the worship and praise of our Redeemer and Creator. In Paul, therefore, our worship is as Trinitarian as our experience of God and our theology. Obviously, it is the presence of the Spirit among us as we gather in Christ's name that makes it so.

---

2. This happens throughout the Psalter. See, e.g., Psalm 30, which offers praise to God in the second person in vv. 1-3, then encourages singing on the part of the "congregation" in vv. 4-5, predicated on the fact that "his favor lasts a lifetime," and returns to second person address in vv. 6-9. Cf. *inter alia* Psalms 32, 66, 104, 116; so also the many hymns that call on the congregation to praise God in light of his character and wondrous deeds.

Chapter 9

Toward a Pauline Theology
of Glossolalia

M ention "salvation by grace alone" and immediately most peo-
    ple think, "the Apostle Paul"; but mention "speaking in
tongues" and most people think, "Pentecostals" or "charismatics."

And this, despite the fact that Paul claims to have spoken in
tongues more than even the Corinthians themselves. This little exercise merely illustrates how much most of us read the New Testament through the filters of our own experience of the church. Moreover, this instinctive way of hearing the word "glossolalia" is
probably unfair both to Paul and to those who currently experience
this (very biblical) expression of Spirituality.[1]

While there are probably many reasons why many contemporary
Christians are uneasy with — or outright reject — this phenomenon
(fear of the unfamiliar, lack of appreciation for anything that is not
overtly rational, some bad experiences with charismatics, etc.), one
of the reasons at least stems from the fact that Pentecostals have

---

1. The capitalization of this word reflects my concerns that this word has bibli-
cal origins, where it is an adjective formed to refer to the work of the Holy Spirit.
On this matter see Fee, *God's Empowering Presence, The Holy Spirit in the Letters of Paul*
(Peabody, MA: Hendrickson, 1994), pp. 28-32, 641-43.

been long on experience in this matter, but sometimes short on theological reflection.[2] Furthermore, the Pentecostal approach to this phenomenon has often had a degree of triumphalism to it that has made it less than attractive to others. Such triumphalism, which is so difficult to square with Pauline theology, has probably led some to discount this form of prayer and praise (1 Cor 14:15-17) as something basically unworthy of Paul himself.

The burden of this paper[3] is to demonstrate that any kind of triumphalistic sense to glossolalia lies outside Paul's own understanding, and that Paul spoke so positively of the gift in 1 Corinthians 14 precisely because it fitted squarely within his overall theology and experience of the Spirit. This is often stated in reverse in the literature, however, as though Paul were merely "damning tongues with faint praise." But such a view is based on a misinterpretation of the Pauline context. What Paul puts down — and unrelentingly so — is the experience of glossolalia in the community when there is no one present to interpret. On the other hand, everything he says about the gift as such, including his own experience of it, is altogether positive. His dictum is unfortunately rarely embraced by many who claim otherwise to follow in his train: "I will do both; I will pray in the Spirit [i.e., in tongues] and I will pray with my understanding."

---

2. This is not altogether true, of course. Much of the older Pentecostal literature had sections that wrestled with "why tongues," or "the value of tongues," which very often took the form of theological reflection; cf. most recently, Robert W. Graves, *Praying in the Spirit* (Old Tappan, NJ: Chosen, 1987), pp. 38-43. I am also well aware that this is not the first attempt at a "theology of glossolalia." See, e.g., J. Massingberd Ford, "Toward a Theology of 'Speaking in Tongues,'" *Theological Studies* 32 (1971): 3-29 (whose journey through Jewish literature led her to an understanding of tongues as God's way of recreating the organ necessary for praise); cf. Frank D. Macchia, "Sighs too Deep for Words: Toward a Theology of Glossolalia," *Journal of Pentecostal Theology* 1 (1992): 47-73. Macchia offers four theological reasons for the gift.

3. The substance of this paper was prepared originally as a contribution to my longtime friend and sometime colleague in the American Assemblies of God, Dr. William W. Menzies; see *Pentecostalism in Context: Essays in Honor of William W. Menzies,* ed. W. Ma and R. P. Menzies (Sheffield: Sheffield Academic Press, 1997), pp. 24-37.

The thesis of this paper is that Paul's understanding of glossolalia is to be found in the paradox of 2 Corinthians 12:9, that "[God's] power finds perfection in [human] weakness," and that speaking in tongues therefore reflects a position of weakness, not of strength. Thus I propose: (1) briefly to overview the theme of power and weakness in Paul; (2) to examine the Pauline data regarding glossolalia from 1 Corinthians; (3) to suggest that these data correspond to Paul's cryptic reference to praying in the Spirit in Romans 8:26-27; and (4) to conclude by showing how these data regarding "prayer in the Spirit" fit into the theme of strength in weakness.

I. THE CONTEXT

One understands Paul and his gospel poorly who does not recognize the crucial role the Spirit plays in his entire theological enterprise;[4] and crucial to the Spirit's central role is the thoroughly eschatological framework within which Paul both experienced and understood the Spirit. The gift of the out-poured Spirit, who had played a fundamental role in his — and others' — eschatological expectations, came to serve for Paul, along with the resurrection of Christ, as the primary cause of his radically altered eschatological perspective. On the one hand, the coming of the Spirit fulfilled the Old Testament eschatological promises, the sure evidence that the future had already been set in motion; on the other hand, since the final expression of the Eschaton had not yet taken place, the Spirit also served as the sure guarantee of the final glory. It is quite impossible to understand Paul's emphasis on the experienced life of the Spirit apart from this thoroughgoing eschatological perspective that dominated his thinking.

It is within this context that one is to understand the inherent ambivalence one finds in Paul's letters between the themes of "power" and "weakness." Indeed, "power" is something of an elusive term in Paul's writings. On the one hand, it often refers to clearly visible manifestations that evidence the Spirit's presence (e.g., 1 Cor

---

4. On this matter see Fee, *Presence,* passim.

2:4-5; Gal 3:5; Rom 15:19). The evidence from 1 Thessalonians 5:19-22; 1 Corinthians 12-14; Romans 12:6; and especially Galatians 3:2-5 with its matter-of-fact appeal to the continuing presence of miracles in the churches, makes it certain that the Pauline churches were "charismatic" in the sense that a dynamic presence of the Spirit was manifested in their gatherings.[5] And even where "power" means that believers apprehend and live out the love of Christ in a greater way (Eph 3:16-20), Paul recognizes here a miraculous work of the Spirit that will be evidenced by the way renewed people behave toward one another. Whatever else, the Spirit was experienced in the Pauline churches; he was not simply a matter of creedal assent.

On the other hand, Paul also assumes the closest correlation between the Spirit's power and present weaknesses. Such passages as Romans 8:17-27; 2 Corinthians 12:9; and Colossians 1:9-11[6] indicate that the Spirit is seen as the source of empowering in the midst of affliction or weakness. In Paul's view, "knowing Christ" means to know "both the power of his resurrection and the fellowship of his sufferings" in which life in the "already" means to be "conformed to his death" as we press toward the "not yet" — the final prize (Phil 3:9-13). This, after all, is almost certainly how we are to understand the double *kai* ("and") that follows "to know him" in this passage. There are not three things that Paul longs to know; rather it is one thing: to know Christ. But in context that means to know him simultaneously in two ways, in both the power of his resurrection and the fellowship of his sufferings.[7] Suffering means to be as one's Lord, following his example and thus "filling up what was lacking in his sufferings" (Col 1:24).

Even so, Paul also expects God's more visible demonstrations of power through the Spirit to be manifested in the midst of weakness,

5. On this matter, see J. D. G. Dunn, *Jesus and the Spirit* (Philadelphia: Westminster, 1975), pp. 260-65; cf. Fee, *Presence*, pp. 894-95.

6. For the exegesis of the passages see Fee, *Presence*, ad loc. In the latter passage Paul prays for the Colossians to be filled with all the Spirit's wisdom and insight so as to walk worthy of Christ, one dimension of which includes "being empowered for endurance and patience with all power in keeping with God's might."

7. Cf. the discussion in Fee, *Paul's Letter to the Philippians* (Grand Rapids: Eerdmans, 1995), pp. 327-36.

as God's "proof" that his power resides in the message of a crucified Messiah. In 1 Corinthians 2:3-5, therefore, Paul can appeal simultaneously to the reality of his own weaknesses and the Spirit's manifest power in his preaching and the Corinthians' conversion; and in 1 Thessalonians 1:5-6 he reminds these new believers that they became so by the power of the Spirit, but in the midst of suffering that was also accompanied by the joy of the Holy Spirit.

All of this reflects Paul's basic eschatological understanding of Christian existence as "already/not yet," a tension that Paul was able to keep together in ways that many later Christians have not. For him it was not simply a tension in which the present was all weakness and the (near) future all glory. The future had truly broken into the present, evidenced by the gift of the Spirit; and since the Spirit meant the presence of God's power, that dimension of the future was also already present in some measure. Thus present suffering is a mark of discipleship, whose paradigm is our crucified Lord. But the same power that raised the crucified One from the dead is also already at work in our present mortal bodies.

It is precisely this paradox in Paul's own understanding that creates so many difficulties for moderns. Indeed, as much as anything else, it is the church's subsequent failure to embrace both power and weakness, simultaneously and vigorously, that has led to so much of the ebb and flow of Spirit life in the church over the centuries. Paul — and the rest of the New Testament writers — held these expressions of Spirit and power in happy tension.[8] Thus Paul in particular steered a path through the "radical middle" that is often missed by both evangelicals and Pentecostals, who traditionally tend to place their emphasis on one side or the other.[9]

I propose in this paper that Paul's stance in the eschatological "radical middle" is the key to his understanding of glossolalia, not

---

8. After all, for Paul the preaching of the crucified One is precisely where God's power is at work in the world (1 Cor 1:18-25), and his own preaching in a context of weakness and fear and trembling certified that the power that brought about the Corinthians' conversion lay in the work of the Spirit, not in the wisdom or eloquence of the preacher.

9. For a further discussion of these two tendencies in the church see *Presence*, pp. 822-26.

simply because he himself stands so squarely over against the Corinthians, whose enchantment with tongues and apparent triumphalism apparently went hand in glove, but also because what Paul says positively about tongues leads in this same direction. Thus we turn once again to a (very) brief examination of the Pauline data.

II. THE PAULINE DATA

It is well known that Paul specifically mentions the phenomenon of glossolalia ("speaking in tongues") only in 1 Corinthians 12–14; it is also generally agreed, although not always in the same way, that Paul's discussion of the phenomenon was primarily for the purpose of correcting a Corinthian abuse, not of instructing them theologically in an area where they needed further teaching. For this reason a certain tenuousness exists for us in the task of theologizing. What we get from Paul are his emphases in correcting the Corinthians rather than full-orbed instruction or reflection.

Nonetheless, several significant conclusions can be drawn from a careful analysis of this section of 1 Corinthians. I simply list them here; they will be elaborated in the next section:

1. Whatever else, glossolalia is Spirit-inspired utterance, as 1 Corinthians 12:7-11 and 14:2 make plain.

2. Whether Paul also understood it to be an actual earthly language is a moot point, but the overall evidence suggests not.

3. It is speech essentially unintelligible both to the speaker (14:14) and to other hearers (14:16), which is why it must be interpreted in the assembly.

4. The regulations for its community use in 14:27-28, plus the declaration in 14:32 that the "Spirit of the prophets is subject to the prophets," make it clear that the speaker is not in "ecstasy" or "out of control."

5. It is speech directed basically toward God (14:2, 14-15, 28), whose content takes the form of prayer, song, blessing (= praise), and thanksgiving.

6. Although he does not forbid its use in the assembly, Paul clearly does not encourage it; rather he insists that they "seek ear-

nestly" to speak what is intelligible to the others, thus to prophesy (14:1, 3-5, 6, 9, 12, 16, 19, 24-25, 28).

7. As a gift for private prayer, Paul held it in the highest regard (14:2, 4a, 15, 17-18). Even though unintelligible to the speaker, such prayer "in the Spirit" edifies the one thus speaking (14:4).

My immediate concern is to point out the significant correspondences between these conclusions (esp. 1, 3, 4, 5, and 7) and what Paul says about "praying in the Spirit" in Romans 8:26-27. In my recent study on the Spirit in Paul, I have argued at length that one can make the best exegetical and phenomenological sense of the Romans passage if we understand the Spirit's making appeal for us "with inarticulate groanings" as referring primarily to glossolalia.[10]

What convinced me to change my mind on this matter[11] was a combination of three realities: (1) The essential matters as to what Paul says about the Spirit's praying through us in Romans 8:26-27 correspond precisely with his description of praying in tongues in 1 Corinthians 14:14-19, namely: (a) that the Spirit is understood to be praying in/through the believer (cf. items 1, 4, and 5 above); and (b) that the one so praying does not understand with his or her mind what the Spirit is saying (cf. items 2, 3, and 7). (2) The experience which Paul describes in Romans 8:26-27 as "the Spirit's interceding with *alalētos* groanings" is expressed in such a way that he is obviously appealing to something that is commonplace among early believers (after all, in this case he is writing to a church that knows him only by reputation, not in person). But in fact there is no other evidence of any kind in the New Testament — or beyond — for such a phenomenon. Glossolalia, on the other hand, has all the earmarks of being commonplace.[12] (3) In that case Paul's use of the

---

10. See *Presence,* pp. 575-86.

11. Cf. my article on the "Pauline Literature" in Stanley M. Burgess and Gary B. McGee, eds., *The Dictionary of Pentecostal and Charismatic Movements* (Grand Rapids: Zondervan, 1988), pp. 665-83 (esp. p. 680).

12. To those who point to its mention only in 1 Corinthians as evidence that it was more or less a strictly Corinthian phenomenon, I point out (a) that only in 1 Corinthians, where he is also correcting an abuse, does Paul mention the Lord's Table(!), and (b) that the nature of Paul's argument in 1 Corinthians 12–14, just as in 11:17-34, assumes a widely known and practiced phenomenon, which was out of

phrase *stenagmos alalētos* (probably = "inarticulate groanings") rather than "glossolalia" (if that is the phenomenon being described in this way) is purely contextual, having been dictated by what he has previously said in vv. 22-23 about the present "groaning" of creation as it awaits the "not yet" of final redemption and of believers "joining with creation" in that "groaning." Thus, despite his use of *alalētos*,13 Paul almost certainly does not intend to describe silent praying, but praying that is "too deep for words" in the sense of "the ordinary words of the speaker's native language." It is therefore "inarticulate" not in the sense that one does not "mouth words,"[14] but in the sense that what is said is not understood by the mind of the speaker.

In any case, what Paul describes in Romans 8:26-27 is clearly a form of "praying in the Spirit," the language he also uses for "speaking in tongues" in 1 Corinthians 14:15-16.[15] Thus, in light of these correspondences, our attempt at theologizing this phenomenon will embrace the data from both passages and should therefore be understood as "toward a theology of praying in the Spirit" — which for Paul would most often have been "in tongues." After all, he can say without proof, but also without fear of contradiction, that "I speak [pray] in tongues more than all of you" to a congregation that

---

control in Corinth. After all, although obviously tailored to their situation, 1 Corinthians 14:26 gives expression to Christian worship that has all the earmarks of being broadly, not locally, conceived. Here, I might add, is the significance of the spurious ending of Mark (16:9-20), an ending which reflects very early tradition, but has no evident association with Corinth. In a quite matter-of-fact way this early tradition says, among other things, that "they will speak in new tongues."

13. By derivation this word literally means "unspoken"; it is quite unlikely that it also means "inexpressible [= too deep for words]," since there is a perfectly good Greek word for that idea (*aneklalētos*; cf. 1 Pet 1:8; Polycarp 1:3). In the context of Romans the word can hardly mean "silent"; therefore, "inarticulate," meaning "without known words," seems to be the best option in this passage.

14. All the more so when one realizes that both praying and reading in antiquity were articulated in the sense of "mouthing the words"; hence they both prayed and read "aloud," as it were.

15. Cf. A. J. M. Wedderburn, "Romans 8:26 — Towards a Theology of Glossolalia?" *SJT* 28 (1975): 369-77, who rejects this interpretation of Romans 8:26 (at least in the form it is presented by E. Käsemann), but allows that it still might function as a basis for a Pauline theology of glossolalia.

has (apparently) taken special pride in the public expression of this phenomenon (1 Cor 14:18).

III. A THEOLOGICAL PROPOSAL

Although Paul does not himself offer theological reflection on the phenomenon of speaking in tongues, what he does say — and to a degree what he does not say — allows us to make several significant affirmations as to his understanding of it. Picking up on the conclusions noted above, I offer the following reflections:

1. That Paul understood glossolalia as Spirit-inspired utterance is clearly expressed in the combination of statements in 1 Corinthians 12:7-8, 10, and 11. In 12:7 he begins by saying that "to each is given the manifestation of the Spirit for the common good," which is followed in vv. 8-10 by a listing of nine such "manifestations," the first four of which are explicitly attributed to the Spirit in such a way ("to one . . . through the Spirit," "to another . . . by the same Spirit") so as to imply that the final five are to be understood in the same way. This is made certain by the wrap-up sentence in v. 11: "All these things the one and the same Spirit works [among you], distributing to each one just as he wills."

This is also explicitly stated in 1 Corinthians 14:2, where Paul affirms that "the one who speaks in tongues . . . speaks mysteries [to God] by the Spirit,"[16] which is then picked up in v. 15 as "I will pray/ sing with my S/spirit."[17] Such praying "by the Spirit" which is unintelligible to the speaker but effective with God is also explicitly stated in Romans 8:26-27.

This theological reality in itself should cause some to speak more cautiously when trying to "put tongues in their place" (usually meaning "to eliminate them altogether") in the contemporary

16. In one of their less insightful moments, the NIV translators, against the clear usage in context and Pauline usage in general, translated this occurrence of *pneumati* as "with his spirit." For Pauline usage in this regard, see chap. 2 in Fee, *Presence*, pp. 15-26.

17. For this translation and understanding of this passage, see Fee, *Presence*, pp. 228-33.

church. Paul does not damn tongues with faint praise, as some have argued, nor does he stand in awe of the phenomenon, as apparently the Corinthians had done — and some later Pentecostals and charismatics as well. As with all Spirit-empowered activity, Paul held it in high regard in its proper place.

2. About the actual phenomenon itself, two things need to be noted. First, the regulations for its community use in 1 Corinthians 14:27-28 make it clear that the speaker is not in "ecstasy" or "out of control." Quite the opposite; the speakers are instructed to speak in turn, one at a time, and they must remain silent if there is no one to interpret. Such instruction makes little or no sense if the speaker is in a kind of "ecstasy" whereby one is understood to be under the "power of the Spirit" and thus out of personal control. What Paul says of prophecy in v. 32, therefore, applies equally to those who would speak in tongues in the assembly: "The S/spirits of the prophets are subject to the prophets." This also means that the outsiders who would view the believers as "mad" if all speak in tongues (simultaneously, seems to be implied) in their gatherings, do not see the "madness" in the nature of the activity itself (= "mania," etc.) but in its lack of intelligibility and lack of order. Likewise, although Paul does not speak to this issue as such in Romans 8:26-27, there is nothing in that description that implies that the speaker is "out of control."

Second, that Paul did not think of glossolalia as an actual earthly language is indicated by several pieces of converging evidence. He certainly does not envisage the likelihood of someone's being present who might understand without interpretation; and the analogy of earthly language in 14:10-12 implies that it is not an earthly language (a thing is not usually identical with that to which it is merely analogous). Our most likely entrée into Paul's understanding is to be found in his description of the phenomenon in 1 Corinthians 13:1 as "the tongues of angels." The context itself demands that this phrase refers to glossolalia. The more difficult matter is its close conjunction with "the tongues of people." Most likely this refers to two kinds of glossolalia: human speech, inspired of the Spirit, but unknown to the speaker or hearers; and angelic speech, inspired of the Spirit to speak in the heavenly dialect. The historical context in general suggests that the latter is what the Corinthians themselves understood glossolalia to be, and therefore considered it one of the evidences of their having already achieved something of their future heavenly status.[18]

3. According to all the available evidence, Paul understood glossolalia as speech directed toward God, not toward other believers. This comes out in a variety of ways. First, this is expressly said in every case where Paul explicitly refers to the direction of the speaking, and in one case this is said in specific contrast to prophecy, which is directed toward other people. Thus in 1 Corinthians 14:2 Paul says that the one who speaks in a tongue does not speak to people, but to God. Likewise in 14:28, if no one is present to interpret the tongue, the speaker is to keep silent in the church and to "speak by him- or herself and to God." The same is implied in vv. 14-16, where the one speaking in tongues is said variously to be "praying" (vv. 14-15), "blessing God" (v. 16), and "giving thanks" (to God, is implied, v. 17). So also, finally, in Romans 8:26-27 the Spirit is presented as praying to God through the believer on the believer's behalf.

Two important considerations arise out of this reality. First, there seems to be little Pauline evidence for the traditional Pentecostal phrase, "a message in tongues," to describe the phenomenon of tongues and interpretation as it has been practiced historically in Pentecostal churches. This language apparently was based on 1 Corinthians 14:5,[19] where Paul gives equal value to prophecy and an interpreted tongue for edifying the believing community. But it

18. The question as to whether the "speaking in tongues" in contemporary Pentecostal and charismatic communities is the same in kind as that in the Pauline churches is moot — and probably somewhat irrelevant. There is simply no way to know. As an experienced phenomenon, it is at the very least analogous to theirs, meaning that it is understood to be a supernatural activity of the Spirit which functions in many of the same ways, and for many of its practitioners has value similar to that described by Paul.

19. See, e.g., Riggs, *The Spirit Himself*, p. 87: "tongues and interpretation are the equivalent of prophecy." He then goes on to offer a considerable apologetic, in light of this assertion, as to why there should be both prophecy and interpreted tongues in the assembly. This is a less common view among more recent Pentecostals; see, e.g., Stanley M. Horton, *What the Bible Says about the Holy Spirit* (Springfield: Gospel Publishing House, 1976).

seems to have been a reading into the text what is not there so as to suggest that prophecy and interpreted tongues thereby become equatable phenomena, since vv. 2 and 28 make it clear that they are not. This is especially so in v. 28 where Paul argues that there must be no glossolalia without interpretation in the church; rather the speaker is told to speak "by himself and to God." The clear implication is that what is interpreted in every case is the speech that in v. 2 is called "speaking mysteries to God." To be sure, one cannot thereby demonstrate that public speaking in tongues is never directed toward the community; what one can say is that Paul never says or implies that it is.

Second, all of the available data, therefore, also indicate that while Paul will not forbid interpreted glossolalia in the assembly, neither is he enthusiastic about it. This is made evident by his explicit preference for prophecy in the church, as well as by the clear implication in 1 Corinthians 14:18-19 ("I speak in tongues more than all of you, but in church five intelligible words are preferable to thousands that are unintelligible") and 28 (to the one speaking in tongues, "if there is no one to interpret remain silent in church and speak to God by yourself").

4. That leads us to note further — and to isolate specifically for the sake of our theological reflections that follow — that the reason for "silence" in church with regard to uninterpreted glossolalia vis-à-vis prophecy is that in both cases Paul's concern is with edification. What happens in the gathered community must be intelligible, precisely so that it can edify the rest of the community. Thus, in the case of uninterpreted glossolalia, the one speaking in tongues "thanks God" to be sure, but the rest of the community cannot be edified and thus say the "Amen" (1 Cor 14:16-17), because they are unable to understand what is being said to God.

But the opposite prevails for the individual believer who prays in tongues in the private place. Such a person "speaks mysteries to God," and even though the mind is at rest and thus unfruitful, it is not detached or out of control. On the contrary, such prayer is a means of edification for the one so praying (1 Cor 14:4) — despite the "unfruitfulness" regarding one's own understanding of what is being said.

While such an understanding runs counter to the heavily Enlightenment-influenced self-understanding of Western Christendom, Romans 8:27 offers the theological key to such edification. It is a matter of trusting God that the One to whom we thus pray by the Spirit "knows the mind of the Spirit, that the Spirit is praying on behalf of the saints what is according to God" [= in keeping with his purposes]. Paul is obviously at rest much more than later Christendom with the Spirit's edifying one's spirit, without such edification needing to be processed in the cortex of the brain. And it is at this point where our final, more theological, reflection emerges, as an attempt to tie parts 1 and 3 of this paper together.

5. The Pauline context for "praying in the Spirit," and thus for glossolalia, is his thoroughgoing eschatological framework, in which he understands the Spirit as the certain evidence that the future has already made its appearance in the present[20] and the sure guarantee of its final consummation.[21] Within this framework glossolalia for Paul serves the believer not as evidence that the future is already present (vis-à-vis Corinth), but that the future is "not yet" consummated.[22] It is because of our "between the times" existence that we desperately need the Spirit's help in our present frailty. This is quite the point of Romans 8:26-27. The Spirit comes alongside, prays through us with "inarticulate groanings," as our help in this present time of weakness. At the same time glossolalia serves as a

20. On this matter see esp. Fee, *Presence*, pp. 803-13. The Spirit is both the "down payment" and the "firstfruits" of the future that has already dawned with the prior coming of Christ and his resurrection and subsequent gift of the eschatological Spirit.

21. See esp. Ephesians 4:30; cf. Fee, "Some Exegetical and Theological Reflections on Ephesians 4:30 and Pauline Pneumatology," in *Spirit and Renewal, Essays in Honor of J. Rodman Williams* (JPTSS 5; Sheffield: Academic Press, 1994), pp. 129-44.

22. Whether or not the Corinthians understood tongues as "showy" is debatable; only the second application of the body analogy in 1 Corinthians 12:22-24 would seem to suggest as much. That they considered tongues as evidence that they had already achieved something of their heavenly status seems much more in keeping with the Pauline argument. But in either case, their view of glossolalia and its purposes was dead wrong from Paul's point of view. Praying in tongues belongs primarily in the privacy of one's own life of prayer; and such "inarticulate groanings" reflect God's power at work even in our present weakness.

constant reminder that we, along with the whole of creation, continue to anticipate our final redemption.

This is why tongues, as well as prophecy and all other Spirit charismata, are for the present time only (1 Cor 13:8-13). Tongues — and prophecy and knowledge — belong to this time of present weakness, when we "know in part" and need the Spirit's help. The believers' praying in tongues echoes the "groaning" of the whole creation, while together we await the final consummation of the future that God has already ushered in by the Resurrection and the gift of the Spirit.

The theological implications of such an understanding are large. In contrast to what is often implied in Pentecostal and charismatic circles, for Paul one does not "pray in tongues" from a position of "strength," as though being filled with the Spirit put one in a position of power before God. Rather, one prays in tongues from a position of weakness, because we "do not know how to pray as we ought." At such times we desperately need the Spirit to help us, for the Spirit to pray through us what is in keeping with God's purposes. And we need especially to learn the kind of trust that such praying inherently demands, namely that God does indeed know the mind of the Spirit, that his intercession for us is right on in terms of God's own purposes in our lives and in the world.

Such an understanding of glossolalia implies weakness in yet another way. Although the one speaking in tongues is not "out of control" in the ecstatic sense of such phenomena, one is not "in control" in the more biblical sense: of giving up control of one's life and agendas, so as to put one's whole self — especially that most unruly part of oneself, the mind and the tongue — at God's disposal,[23] be-

---

23. I admit to wondering at times whether present resistance to glossolalia on the part of so many is not a combination of both a misunderstanding of Paul's own perspective on this matter and of our need to be "in control." Maybe the bottom line of such resistance is our lip-service to putting ourselves at God's disposal in our weakness, but insisting that all of our praying should be from a stance of strength — the form of strength found in our praying only with our minds and seldom in the Spirit. This is another place where cessationism fails — in all its forms. Not only is it exegetically and hermeneutically unsupportable, but it ends up being a form of "living from a position of strength," in this case in the strength of a rationalistic mind-set.

lieving that his love for us is absolutely pure, totally "without dissimulation" (to use an old King James phrase), and that he purposes only good for "the saints." This is why Paul insists that he will do both: that he will pray and sing with his mind (for the sake of others), and that he will pray and sing in the Spirit (for his own sake).

At the same time, by thus praying out of a stance of weakness, Paul also affirms our utter dependence upon God for all things; and here is where the "power in weakness" comes in. By praying through us in tongues, the Spirit is the way whereby God's strength is made perfect in the midst of our weakness — which is where the ultimate strength lies for the believer. Thus our praying in tongues, while evidence for us that we have entered the new, eschatological age ushered in by the Spirit, serves especially as evidence that we are still "not yet" regarding the consummation of that age. Because we have not yet arrived, and await with the whole of creation our final redemption, we thus pray in the Spirit out of weakness, implicitly trusting the Spirit to pray in keeping with God's purposes. Such praying is thus freedom and power, God's power being perfected in the midst of our weakness.

I note finally that if the view presented here is in fact faithful to Paul, one can also understand why, on the one hand, he speaks so little of it, but speaks so positively of it, on the other; and why also he himself was given to it in his private praying far more than any of the Corinthians who appeared to prize it so highly. Paul's entire understanding of present existence in Christ by the Spirit is one in which God's power and wisdom are best exhibited through human weakness and frailty. This is why he refused to know anything among the Corinthians except "Christ and him crucified"; this is why he argues with them as he does in 2 Corinthians 11–12; and this is why he can speak so confidently of the Spirit's empowering even while he himself knows weakness, suffering, imprisonment, scoffing.

In sum, understood from Paul's perspective, speaking in tongues fits the whole of his theological outlook. Here is our opportunity to express our deepest selves to God — in praise, thanksgiving, prayer, and intercession. And this is so especially when we do not ourselves know what to pray in the midst of present weakness; but what we do know, Paul goes on, is that by thus praying on our behalf in our present weakness, "the Spirit works all things together for good, for us who love God and are called in keeping with God's purposes" (Rom 8:28).[24]

24. For this understanding of this familiar passage, see Fee, *Presence*, pp. 587-90.

Chapter 10

Laos *and Leadership*
under the New Covenant

The New Testament is full of surprises, but perhaps none so much as with its generally relaxed attitude toward church structures and leadership; especially so, when one considers how important this issue became for so much of later church history, beginning as early as Ignatius of Antioch. Indeed, for most people the concept of "church history" refers primarily to its history as a body politic, involving both its evangelism and growth and its intellectual/theological development.

This paper was originally prepared for discussion at a Regent College faculty retreat. Rather than a research paper that tries to take account of the vast array of secondary literature (on church order and laity), I have attempted something more modest: an essay that offers one New Testament scholar's reading of the biblical texts on specific issues related to the church as the people of God, namely, the interrelationships between people, clergy, ministry, and church order. Although what I do here is akin to reinventing the wheel, hopefully some items will be fresh — although on others I can be easily scored for not having consulted the literature.

I am grateful to my Regent colleagues for a vigorous discussion of the paper, from which I have made a few small revisions and added some footnotes for greater clarity.

Probably for a variety of reasons,[1] the New Testament documents simply do not carry a concern for church order as an agendum.[2] The thesis of this paper is that the *primary* reason for this stems from their understanding of what it means to be the people of God under a new covenant, as that in turn is related to their common experience of the eschatological Spirit.[3] The burden of the paper is ultimately hermeneutical — how we move from the first-century documents to twentieth (twenty-first) century application. But those questions, as always, must first be subject to the exegetical ones — how we understand the texts themselves.

---

1. One reason not otherwise noted in this paper is the especially *ad hoc* nature of our documents. Even the so-called Pastoral Epistles show little interest in church leadership or governance as such. Rather Paul is concerned with the character and qualifications of those who assume positions of leadership. See G. D. Fee, *1 and 2 Timothy, Titus* (Peabody, MA: Hendrickson, 1988), pp. 19-23, 78-79.

2. As I have noted elsewhere, the very fact that such diverse groups as Roman Catholics, Plymouth Brethren, and Presbyterians all use the Pastoral Epistles to support their ecclesiastical structures should give us good reason to pause as to what the New Testament "clearly teaches" on these matters. See "Reflections on Church Order in the Pastoral Epistles, with Further Reflection on the Hermeneutics of Ad Hoc Documents," *Journal of the Evangelical Theological Society* 28 (1985): 141-51.

This is one of the things that make Acts such a different kind of "church history" from its successors. There is scarcely a hint of church organization or structures (1:15-26 and 6:1-6 play quite different roles). At some point, for example, leadership in Jerusalem passed from the Twelve to James (cf. 6:2 and 8:14 with 11:2; 12:17; and 15:13), without so much as a word as to how or why. At the local level, in 13:13, those who appear to be in leadership are "prophets and teachers," while in 14:23 elders are appointed for each congregation. This is hardly the stuff from which one can argue with confidence as to how the early church was "organized" — or whether it was!

3. By this I mean something quite technical, namely the outpouring of the promised Holy Spirit as the primary reality indicating that Jewish eschatological hopes had been fulfilled, or realized. For the early church "this is that which was spoken by the prophet Joel" (Acts 2:16), the sure evidence that the End *(Eschaton)* had begun and the time of the Future had dawned.

1. THE ISSUE(S)

Historically the church seems to have fallen into[4] a model that eventually developed a sharp distinction between the people themselves (laity) and the professional ministry (clergy), reaching its sharpest expression in the Roman Catholic communion,[5] but finding its way into almost every form of Protestantism as well. The net result has been a church in which the clergy all too often exist apart from the people, for whom there is a different set of rules and different expectations, and a church in which the "gifts" and "ministry," not to mention significance, power structures, and decision-making, are the special province of the professionals. Being "ordained" to this profession, the latter tend to like the aura that it provides, and having such ordained professionals allows the laity to pay them to do the work of the ministry and thus excuse themselves from their biblical calling. The rather universal model, with a few exceptions, looks something like this:

The thesis of this paper is that the biblical model looks something more like the following diagram — without clergy at all, but with identifiable leadership, who were simply part of the whole people of God:

4. In contrast to having come by such order through purposeful, intentional action on its part.

5. I mean *de jure*, of course. One of my colleagues pointed out that *de facto* there is nothing more severe in this regard than some independent churches (baptist, pentecostal/charismatic).

The problem for most moderns, of course, in coming to the biblical texts, is that we tend to presuppose our resultant form of church to be theirs; we therefore carry both different agenda and a different experience of the church back to the documents. But history and tradition have had their innings. Even though it is arguable that we have genuine continuity with the New Testament church in many ways — especially our experience of grace and the Spirit — our experience of the church itself is so far different from theirs that seemingly ne'er the twain shall meet.[6]

As I see it, the areas of difficulty are four: (1) the tension between individual and corporate life, where western Christians in particular are trained from birth to value the individual above the group, whereas in the New Testament perspective the community is still the primary reality, and the individual finds identity and meaning as part of the community; (2) the tension between eschatological and institutional existence, most moderns knowing only the latter, whereas the New Testament church existed primarily as an experience of the former; (3) the place of structures as they flow out of these two tensions; and (4) the hermeneutical difficulty created by the nature of data, since the New Testament documents, which teem with reflections and insights, have very little directly intentional instruction on these matters. So how do they apply? Do we seek a biblical norm to follow,[7] or seek to model what fits our situation best, or try rather to approximate the spirit of the biblical pattern in our already existing structures?

---

6. For me this is always brought home as a living reality in teaching New Testament theology. Although my emphases and packaging of the biblical data frequently stimulate rousing discussion (debate?), nothing does so quite as much as the section in Pauline theology on the nature of the church as the eschatological people of God, presently living out the life of the future as they await the consummation. Not only do I have great difficulty in helping students to catch the New Testament perspective, but even when it happens, there is difficulty in assimilating it — because this touches them right where they live.

7. Whether we should try to model the New Testament church, of course, is yet another hermeneutical question in its own right. On the place of "historical precedent" in Christian hermeneutics, see some programmatic suggestions in G. D. Fee and D. Stuart, *How to Read the Bible for All Its Worth*, 2nd ed. (Grand Rapids: Zondervan, 1993), pp. 94-112.

I propose in the rest of this paper to take up some of these issues by first examining the biblical data and then by offering some brief hermeneutical observations in light of those data.

2. THE PEOPLE OF GOD IN THE NEW TESTAMENT

2.1. *The Language*

By first pursuing the New Testament language for the Christian communities, I hope to demonstrate two realities about them: (a) their strong sense of *continuity* with the people of God under the former covenant, and (b) their basically *corporate* nature.

That the early believers thought in terms of continuity is writ large on nearly every page, in nearly every document.[8] They did not see themselves as the "*new* people of God," but as the "people of God *newly constituted.*" Nowhere is this more clear than in their adopting Old Testament "people of God" language, a language appropriation that is as varied as it is thoroughgoing.

2.1.1. Church *(ekklesia)*

Because this word does not appear in the English Old Testament, and because its usage for the "assembly" of the Greek *polis* is generally well known, the Old Testament background for New Testament usage is frequently overlooked. In the LXX *ekklesia* is regularly used to translate the Hebrew *qahal,* referring most often to the "congregation of Israel," especially when it was gathered for religious purposes.[9] Thus this word in particular was a natural one for the early

---

8. This is no more than we should expect, given Jesus as the fulfillment of Jewish messianic expectations, his own announcement of the kingdom as "fulfilling the time," and the Jewish complexion of the earliest believers. Continuity is thus found in a whole variety of ways in the Gospels: e.g., in direct statements reflecting the motif of promise and fulfillment, in symbols and images of various kinds (Jesus' choice of the Twelve is scarcely accidental!), in the hymns in Luke's birth narrative.

9. Thus, e.g., Deuteronomy 31:30: "And Moses recited the words of this song from the beginning to end in the hearing of the whole *ekklesia* of Israel."

believers to bridge the gap as they began to spill over into the Gentile world.

Since the concept of a "gathered people" was primary in both Greek and LXX usage, it is arguable that this is what lay behind the earliest Christian usage as well. Thus in its first appearance in the New Testament (1 Thess 1:1) Paul is probably thinking primarily of the Christian community as a gathered people, constituted "in God the Father and the Lord Jesus Christ," who would be listening to the letter as it was read. It is also arguable that its usage throughout the New Testament never gets very far away from this nuance; the *ekklesia* refers first of all to the people in the various cities and towns who gather regularly in the name of the Lord for worship and instruction.

2.1.2. People *(laos)*

Although not particularly popular with Greek writers, this is the word chosen by the LXX translators[10] to render the Hebrew *'am*, the word that occurs most often (over 2000 times) to express the special relationship Israel had with Yahweh: Above all else they were Yahweh's "people." Although at times the word can distinguish the people (usually non-Israelite) from their leaders (e.g., Gen 41:40; Exod 1:22), in most cases it is the collective word that designates the whole people whom God had chosen — people, priests, prophets, and kings together. Thus in Exodus 19:5, in establishing his covenant with them at Sinai, God says (LXX), "You shall be for me a *laos periousios* (special/chosen people) from among the *ethnōn* (nations/Gentiles)."

In the New Testament the word occurs most often to refer to the Jewish people of that era.[11] But in several striking passages it is used in its Old Testament sense, especially reflecting the language of Exo-

10. Probably because the more common word *ethnos* was used by Greek writers to refer to themselves as a people in the same way the Hebrews used *'am*. Thus for the Jews *ethnos* came to = "gentiles," and was so used by the LXX translators. Hence the need for a different word to distinguish themselves.

11. Luke uses it most often (84 of 142); Matthew, 14; Hebrews, 13; Paul, 12; Revelation, 9. In many of these it occurs in citations of the Old Testament.

dus 19:5-6 (cf. 23:22 LXX), to refer to people of the new covenant, usually in contexts that include Gentiles. Thus Luke reports James as saying: "How God at first showed his concern by taking from the *ethnōn* a *laos* for his name" (Acts 15:14); in Titus 2:14 the goal of Christ's saving purpose is "that he might purify for himself a *laos periousios*," while 1 Peter 2:9-10 combines "people" language from two Old Testament passages (Isa 43:20; Exod 19:6; Isa 43:21), followed by a wordplay on Hosea 2:25 (cf. 1:9), to designate Gentile Christians as "a chosen people, a royal priesthood, a holy nation, a people belonging to God," who were formerly "no people" but now "are the people of God." So also the author of Hebrews transfers several Old Testament "people" passages or concepts to the church (2:17; 4:9; 7:27; 13:12).

2.1.3. Covenant *(diatheke)*

Although this term does not occur often in the New Testament, it is used in ways that are significant to our topic. The author of Hebrews in particular adopts covenantal language to tie the new to the old, seeing Christ as the fulfillment of Jeremiah's "new covenant" in which God says again, as in the Sinaitic covenant, "They shall be for me a people" (Heb 8:7-12; citing Jer 31:34). Paul also adopts this language to refer to the "new covenant" of the Spirit (2 Cor 3:6; cf. Gal 4:24). Perhaps even more significantly, as the people joined in common fellowship at the Table of the Lord in the Pauline churches, they did so with these words: "This cup is the new covenant in my blood" (1 Cor 11:25; Luke 22:20). It should be noted that both the language "new covenant" and its close tie with the Spirit and the people of God are seen in terms of continuity with the Old Testament (in this case as fulfillment); thus in the church's earliest worship and liturgy there was the constant reminder of their continuity/discontinuity with the past.[12]

12. Just as the Table, through its symbol of the bread (1 Cor 10:16-17), should serve for us as a reminder of our continuity with centuries of believers.

2.1.4. Saints *(hoi hagioi)*

Although not frequent in the Old Testament, the designation of Israel as God's "holy people" occurs in the crucial covenantal passage in Exodus 19:5-6, an expression that in later Judaism referred to the elect who were to share in the blessings of the messianic kingdom (Dan 7:18-27; Ps. Sol. 17; Qumran). This is Paul's primary term for God's newly formed, eschatological people. He uses it in the salutation of six of the nine letters addressed to congregations, plus Philemon, as well as in several other kinds of settings. Its appearance in Acts 9:41; Hebrews 6:10; 13:24; Jude 3; and Revelation 8:4 makes it clear that this was widespread usage in the early church. In all cases it is a designation for the collective people of God, who are to bear his "holy" character and thus to be "set apart" for his purposes. To put that another way, the New Testament knows nothing about individual "saints," only about Christian communities as a whole who take up the Old Testament calling of Israel to be "God's holy people" in the world.[13]

2.1.5. Chosen (*eklektos* and Cognates)

Closely related to the covenant is the concept of Israel as having been chosen by God, by an act of sheer mercy on his part. In the Old Testament this concept is most often found in verb form, with God as the subject. However, the LXX of Isaiah 43:20-21 uses *eklektos* as a designation for the restored people of God. This usage is picked up in several places in the New Testament (e.g., Mark 13:22; 1 Thess 1:4; 2 Thess 2:13; Col 3:12; Eph 1:4, 11; 1 Peter 1:2; 2:9). As in the Old Testament the term does not refer to individual election, but to a people who have been chosen by God for his purposes; as one has been incorporated into, and thus belongs to, the chosen people of God, one is in that sense also elect. Also as in the Old Testament, this language places the ultimate ground of our being in a sovereign and gracious God, who willed and initiated salvation for his people.

13. See G. D. Fee, *The First Epistle to the Corinthians* (Grand Rapids: Eerdmans, 1987), pp. 32-33, for the difficulties in rendering this term into English; the option which seems best to capture its inherent nuances is "God's holy people."

2.1.6. Royal Priesthood

This term, taken directly from Exodus 19:6, is used in 1 Peter 2:9-10 to refer to the church. I include it here not only because it is further demonstration of continuity, but also because as in the Exodus passage it so clearly refers to the people corporately,[14] not to individual priests, nor to the priesthood of individual believers.[15]

2.1.7. The Israel of God

This unique expression occurs only in Galatians 6:16 in the entire Bible. Nonetheless, in many ways it gathers up much of the New Testament thinking — especially Paul's — on this matter. All those who live by the "rule" that neither circumcision nor uncircumcision counts for anything, these are "the Israel of God" upon whom God's benediction of shalom and mercy now rests.[16] While it is true that Paul does not call the church the "new Israel," such passages as Romans 2:28-29; 9:5; Philippians 3:3, and this one demonstrate that Paul saw the church as the "true Israel," i.e., as in the true succession of the Old Testament people of God. At the same time it emphasizes that those people are now newly constituted — composed of Jew and Gentile alike, and based solely on faith in Christ and the gift of the Spirit.

This comes through nowhere more forcefully than in the argument of Galatians itself, for which this passage serves as the climax.

---

14. Cf. B. Childs on Exodus 19:6: "Israel as a people is also dedicated to God's service among the nations as priests function with a society" (*The Book of Exodus* [Philadelphia: Westminster, 1974], p. 367).

15. The New Testament knows nothing of the "priesthood of the believer" as it is popularly conceived, with each person's being his or her own priest with God, without need of an external priesthood. To the contrary, the New Testament teaches that the church has a priestly function for the world (1 Peter 2:9-10); and our role of ministering to one another makes us priests one for another.

16. Although it is grammatically possible that this phrase refers to Jewish people, and is so argued by many (see esp. P. Richardson, *Israel in the Apostolic Church* [Society for New Testament Studies Monograph Series 10: Cambridge University Press, 1969], pp. 74-102), both the unusual nature of the qualifier "of God" and the context of the whole argument argue for the position taken here.

Paul's concern throughout has been to argue that through Christ and the Spirit Gentiles share with believing Jews full privileges in the promises made to Abraham (indeed are Abraham's true children), without submitting to Torah in the form of Jewish identity symbols (circumcision, food laws, calendar observance).[17] They do not need to submit to the regulations of the old covenant in order to be full members of the people of God; indeed in "belonging to Christ," they are "Abraham's seed, and heirs according to the promise" (3:29), which is confirmed for them by the gift the Spirit (4:6-7).

Here especially the primary name for God's ancient people has been taken over in the interests of continuity, but now predicated on new terms. The Israel *of God* includes both Jew and Gentile, who by faith in Christ and "adoption" by the Spirit, have become Abraham's "free children," and through Christ the inheritors of the promises made to Abraham. Gentile believers *as a people* are included in the newly constituted people of God, the Israel of God, which is at the same time also an obviously corporate image.

2.1.8. Further (non-Old Testament) Images

The essentially corporate nature of the people of God is further demonstrated by the various images for the church found in the New Testament that are not from the Old Testament: *family,* where God is Father and his people are brothers and sisters; the related image of *household,* where the people are members of the household (1 Tim 3:5, 15) and their leaders the Master's servants (1 Cor 4:1-3); *body,* where the emphasis is simultaneously on their unity and diversity (1 Cor 10:17; 12:12-26); God's *temple,* or sanctuary, where by the Spirit they corporately serve as the place of God's

---

17. The issue in Galatians is not first of all justification by faith (i.e., entrance requirements), but whether Gentiles, who have already been justified by faith in Christ and given the Spirit must also submit to Jewish boundary markers (i.e., maintenance requirements) in order to share in the covenant with Abraham (as Genesis 17:1-14 makes so clear). For arguments presenting this perspective see T. David Gordon, "The Problem in Galatia," *Interpretation* 41 (1987): 32-43; and J. D. G. Dunn, "The Theology of Galatians," *Society of Biblical Literature 1988 Seminar Papers* (Atlanta: Scholars Press, 1988), pp. 1-16.

dwelling (1 Cor 3:16-17; 2 Cor 6:16; Eph 2:21-22); God's *commonwealth,* where as citizens of heaven Jew and Gentile alike form a *polis* in exile, awaiting their final homeland (Phil 3:20-21; Eph 2:19; 2 Peter 1:1, 17).

In sum: By using so much Old Testament language to mark off their own identity, the early church saw themselves not only as in continuity with the Old Testament people of God, but as in the true succession of that people. One of the essential features of this continuity is the corporate nature of the people of God. God chose, and made covenant with, not individual Israelites but with a people, who would bear his name and be for his purposes. Although individual Israelites could forfeit their position in Israel, this never affected God's design or purposes with the people as a people. This is true even when the majority failed, and the "people" were reduced to a "remnant." That remnant was still Israel — loved, chosen, and redeemed by God.

This is the thoroughgoing perspective of the New Testament as well, but at the same time Christ's coming and the gift of the eschatological Spirit also marked a new way by which they were constituted. The community is now entered individually through faith in Christ and the reception of the Spirit, signaled by baptism. Nonetheless, the church itself is the object of God's saving activity in Christ. God is thus choosing and saving a people for his name.

Perhaps nothing illustrates this quite so vividly as two passages in 1 Corinthians (5:1-13; 6:1-11), where rather flagrant sins on the part of individuals are spoken to. In both cases Paul aims his heaviest artillery not at the individual sinners, but at the church for its failure to deal with the matters. In 5:1-13 the man is not so much as spoken to, and his partner is not mentioned at all; everything is directed at the church — for its arrogance, on the one hand, and its failure to act, on the other. So also in 6:1-11. In this case he does finally speak to the plaintiff (vv. 7-8a) and the defendant (vv. 8b-11), but only after he has scored the church for its allowing such a thing to happen at all among God's eschatological community, and thus for its failure to act. What is obviously at stake in these cases is the church itself, and its role as God's redeemed and redemptive alternative to Corinth.

2.2. The People and Their Leadership

The sense of continuity with the old, however, does not seem to carry over to the role of leadership as well. Under the old covenant the king and priests in particular, although often included in much of the "people" language, were at the same time recognized as having an existence apart from the people with their own sets of rules and expectations. It is precisely this model of leadership that breaks down altogether in the New Testament. The basic reason for this is the Lordship of Christ himself. As God intended to be himself king over Israel, so Christ has come as God's king over his newly constituted people. As head of his church, all others, including leaders, function as parts of the body both sustained by Christ and growing up into him (Eph 4:11-16).

Thus leadership in the New Testament people of God is never seen as outside or above the people themselves, but simply as part of the whole, essential to its well-being, but governed by the same set of "rules." They are not "set apart" by "ordination";[18] rather their gifts are part of the Spirit's work among the whole people. That this is the basic model (as diagrammed earlier) can be demonstrated in a number of ways, some of which deserve special attention.

2.2.1. The Nature of the Epistles

One of the more remarkable features of the New Testament Epistles is the twin facts (a) that they are addressed to the church(es) as a whole, not to the church leadership,[19] and (b) that leaders, there-

18. That is, they are not "set apart" to an office; rather hands are laid upon them in recognition of the Spirit's prior activity. Cf. Acts 13:1-2; 1 Timothy 4:4.

19. The one exception to this is Philippians, where Paul writes to the church "together with the overseers and deacons." One might also include Philemon, where Paul includes Archippus in the salutation, but since the letter is addressed to Philemon, Paul continues by mentioning two further individuals before including the church. Some, of course, would argue that 1 Timothy and Titus are such documents; however, both of these younger colleagues serve as Paul's own apostolic delegates in Ephesus and Crete. They are both itinerants, whose stay is temporary. Thus they are not church leaders in the local sense.

fore, are seldom, if ever,[20] singled out either to see to it that the directives of a given letter are carried out or to carry them out themselves.

To the contrary, in every case, the writers address the community as a whole, and the expectation of the letter is that there will be a community response to the directives. In several instances leaders are mentioned (e.g., 1 Thess 5:12-13; 1 Cor 16:16; Heb 13:17), but basically in order to address the community's attitudes toward them. In 1 Peter 5:1-4 the leaders themselves (apparently)[21] are addressed, in this case with regard to their attitudes and responsibilities toward the rest of the people.

Thus, for example, in 1 Thessalonians 5:12-13 the whole community is called upon, among other things, to respect those who labor among them, care for them,[22] and admonish them; yet in vv. 14-15, when urging that they "admonish the idle, encourage the fainthearted, help the weak, be patient with all," Paul is once more addressing the *community as a whole,* not its leadership in particular. So also in 2 Thessalonians 3:14 the whole community is to "note that person" who does not conform to Paul's instruction and "have nothing to do with him." Likewise, in all of 1 Corinthians not one of the many directives is spoken to the leadership, and in 14:26 their worship is singularly corporate in nature ("When you [plural] as-

20. The one exception to this might be Philippians 4:3, where Paul asks a trusted fellow-worker to mediate the differences between Euodia and Syntyche. But more likely, since these two women are also designated as his fellow-workers, he is asking for help not so much from a church leader as such, but from one who has been a co-laborer with both Paul and these women. As in the preceding note, Timothy and Titus are "leaders" of a different kind. They are in their respective situations in Paul's place; they are not local leaders "in charge" of the church.

21. This seems almost certainly to be the case, despite the corresponding "younger men" that follows in v. 5.

22. The verb in this case is ambiguous in Greek, meaning either to "govern" or to "care for." Apart from 1 Timothy 3:4-5, elsewhere in the New Testament, as here, it is used absolutely so that one cannot determine which nuance is intended. But in the Timothy passage the synonym that is substituted for it in v. 5 means unambiguously "to care for." This seems most likely what Paul ordinarily had in mind. Cf. E. Best, *The First and Second Epistles to the Thessalonians* (San Francisco: Harper, 1972), pp. 224-25.

semble together, *each one of you has . . .*; let all things be done with an eye to edification"). One receives the distinct impression that people and leaders alike are under the sovereign direction of the Holy Spirit.

This is not to downplay the role of leadership;[23] rather it is to recognize that in the New Testament documents leaders are always seen as *part of the whole people of God,* never as a group unto themselves. Hence they "labor among" you, Paul repeatedly says, and their task in Ephesians 4:11-16 is especially "to prepare God's people ['the saints'] for works of service ['ministry'], so that the body of Christ may be built up." Thus the model that emerges in the New Testament is not that of clergy and laity, but of the whole people of God, among whom the leaders function in service of the rest.

All of this is quite in keeping with Jesus' word that they are to call no one "rabbi," "father," or "master," for "you have one teacher and you are all brothers and sisters" (Matt 23:8-12), and with his word that "those who are supposed to rule over the Gentiles lord it over them, and their great men exercise authority over them. But it shall not be so among you; but whoever would be great among you must be your servant, and whoever would be first among you must be slave of all" (Mark 10:42-44).

2.2.2. The New Testament Imperatives

Closely related to this is another reality that is easily missed in an individualistic culture, namely that the imperatives in the Epistles are primarily corporate in nature, and have to do first of all with the community and its life together; they address individuals only as they are part of the community. In the early church everything was done *allelōn* ("one another"). They were members of one another

---

23. Indeed, despite some New Testament scholarship to the contrary, it is highly unlikely that the early communities ever existed long without local leadership. The picture Luke gives in Acts 14:23 is an altogether plausible one historically, given the clear evidence of leadership in the earliest of the Pauline letters (1 Thess 5:12-13) — a community where he had not stayed for a long time, whose leadership must have been in place when he was suddenly taken from them (Acts 17:10; 1 Thess 2:17).

(Rom 12:5; Eph 4:25),[24] who were to build up one another (1 Thess 5:11; Rom 14:19), care for one another (1 Cor 12:25), love one another (1 Thess 3:12; 4:9; Rom 13:8; 1 John *passim*), bear with one another in love (Eph 4:2), bear one another's burdens (Gal 6:2), be kind and compassionate to one another, forgiving one another (Eph 4:32), submit to one another (Eph 5:21), consider one another better than themselves (Phil 2:3), be devoted to one another in love (Rom 12:10), and live in harmony with one another (Rom 12:16).

All of the New Testament imperatives are to be understood within this framework. Unfortunately, many texts which Paul intended for the community as a whole have been regularly individualized, thus losing much of their force and impact. For example, in 1 Corinthians 3:10-15 Paul is not talking of believers building their individual lives on Christ; rather the admonition in v. 10 ("let each one take care how he/she builds") is intended precisely for those in Corinth responsible for building the church, that they do it with the imperishable materials compatible with the foundation (a crucified Messiah), not with "wisdom" and division. Likewise vv. 16-17 are a warning to those who would "demolish" God's temple, the church in Corinth, by their divisions and fascination with "wisdom." And on it goes. "Work out your own salvation with fear and trembling, for God is at work in you both to will and to work for his good pleasure" (Phil 2:12-13) is not a word to the individuals in the community to work harder at their Christian lives, but is spoken to a community that is out of sync with one another (as vv. 1-5 make clear) and needs to work out its common salvation with God's help. In the same vein, it is impossible to compute the misunderstandings that have arisen over 1 Corinthians 12–14 because the text has been looked at outside the context of the community at worship.

All of this, then, to say that the people of God in the New Testament are still thought of corporately, and individually only as they are members of the community. And leadership is always seen as

---

24. This is an obvious reference to the imagery of the church as the body of Christ, another corporate image used by Paul, which I have not dealt with in this paper because it is both so obvious and lacking Old Testament roots.

part of the whole complex. Leaders do not exercise authority over God's people — although the community is to respect them and submit to their leadership; rather they are the "servants of the farm" (1 Cor 3:5-9), or "household" (1 Cor 4:1-3). The New Testament is not concerned with their place in the governance structures (hence as we will note below, we know very little about these but with their attitudes and servant nature. They do not rule,[25] but serve and care for — and that within the circle, as it were.

3. THE THEOLOGICAL BASIS FOR THE NEW TESTAMENT PEOPLE OF GOD

Before turning our attention to some observations about the nature of structures and ministry in the New Testament, it is time now to suggest the theological/experiential basis for the New Testament church's *discontinuity* with the old, and thus for their being a newly constituted people, which in turn accounts for their relaxed attitude toward governance structures as such. This basis, I suggest, is a combination of three realities:[26] the work of Christ, the gift of the Spirit, and the eschatological framework within which both of these were understood.

3.1. The Work of Christ

We need not belabor this point. The single, central reality of the New Testament is that "God has made him both Lord and Christ, this Jesus whom you crucified" (Acts 2:36); and that changes everything. On the one hand, he "fulfills" all manner of hopes and expec-

25. Language of "rulership" and "authority" is altogether missing in the New Testament passages which speak about leadership, except as Paul refers to his apostolic authority in his own churches.

26. To be complete and more precise, of course, one should start with their absolutely primary theological presupposition: That the one God — holy, sovereign, and gracious — had purposed their salvation, which he effected in Christ and made available for all through the Spirit (see, e.g., Gal 4:4-7).

136

tations, thus functioning as both continuity and discontinuity with the old: he is the "seed" of Abraham, inheritor of the promises to Abraham, through whom both Jew and Gentile alike are now "heirs according to promise" (Gal 3:16, 29); he is the great high priest, whose singular sacrifice of himself eliminates all other priests and offerings, through whom we all now have direct access to the Father (Hebrews); he is the rejected stone now become the chief cornerstone by whom we have become living stones in God's new "spiritual house" (1 Peter 2:4-8).

On the other hand, the death and resurrection of Christ bring an *end* to the old and begin the new. His death ratified a new covenant, so that the people of God are newly constituted — based on faith in Christ and including Gentile as well as Jew.[27] His resurrection set the future in motion in such a way that this newly constituted people are "raised with him" and enter an entirely new mode of existence — so much so that a radically new understanding of that existence also emerged.

This is obviously the focus of New Testament theology, and the primary reason for discontinuity with the former people of God (in the sense that they must now come through Christ in order to belong). But such focus does not in itself account for the people of God sensing themselves to be a *newly constituted people* as well.[28] This can only be accounted for on the basis of the eschatological framework of their self-understanding and the role of the Spirit within that understanding.

---

27. The classic illustration of Paul's own struggle with continuity and discontinuity between the new and the old — expressed in terms of Gentile and Jew — is Romans 11, where Gentiles have been grafted onto the olive tree "and now share in the nourishing sap from the olive root" (v. 17, NIV). Yet Israel itself must be regrafted in order to be saved.

28. After all, in the early going, as Luke portrays things in Acts 1-6, the early believers lived within Judaism — and surely expected that all Jewry would acknowledge Jesus as Messiah, Savior, and Lord.

3.2. The Gift of the Spirit

Although the New Testament people of God were constituted on the basis of Christ's death and resurrection, the Spirit, who appropriated that work to their lives, was the key to their present existence as that people. The Spirit is both the *evidence* that God's eschatological future had dawned (Acts 2:16-21) and the *guarantee* of their own inheritance at its consummation (Eph 1:13-14).[29]

The Spirit is that which marks off God's people from the rest, whereby they understand the wisdom of the cross, which the world counts as foolishness (1 Cor 2:6-16). Their common experience of Spirit, both Jew and Gentile, plus their continuing experience of the Spirit's activities among them, is that to which Paul appeals in Galatia as evidence of the new expression of being God's people (Gal 3:2-5); and the Spirit by whom they walk, in whom they live, and by whom they are led is the reason they no longer need Torah (5:16-28). Not only has Christ brought an end to Torah but by belonging to him believers have also crucified the flesh (Gal 5:24) that was aroused by Torah (Rom 7:5). Through the Spirit they fulfill the whole Torah as well as the law of Christ by loving one another (Gal 5:13-14; 6:2).

Moreover, the Spirit is the key to their existence as a people. Through Christ both Jew and Gentile together "have access in one Spirit to the Father" (Eph 2:18). By their common, lavish experience

---

29. Cf. the powerful eschatological metaphors of the Spirit in Paul that especially make these double points: "seal" (2 Cor 1:21-22; Eph 1:13; 4:30); "earnest/first installment" (2 Cor 1:21-22; 5:5; Eph 1:14); "firstfruits" (Rom 8:23). This latter metaphor in particular helps us to see how Paul views life in the Spirit as lived in the eschatological tension of the "already" and the "not yet"; while at the same time the Spirit is the guarantee of our certain future. The larger context of Romans 8:12-27 is especially noteworthy. With the Spirit playing the leading role, Paul in vv. 15-17 has struck the dual themes (1) of our present position as children, who are thus joint-heirs with Christ of the Father's glory, and (2) of our present existence as one of weakness and suffering, as we await that glory. These are the two themes taken up in vv. 18-27. By the Spirit we have already received our "adoption" as God's children, but what is "already" is also "not yet"; therefore, by the same Spirit, who functions for us as firstfruits, we await our final "adoption as children," "the redemption of our bodies." The first sheaf is God's pledge to us of the final harvest.

of Spirit the many of them in Corinth, with all their differences and diversity, became the one body of Christ (1 Cor 12:13); by the Spirit's abiding in/among them they form God's temple, holy unto him — set apart for his purposes as his alternative to Corinth (1 Cor 3:16-17).

Finally, the Spirit serves as the key to their new view of ministry. Ministry lies not in individuals with inherited offices, nor even in individuals with newly created offices. Ministry lies with the gifting of the Spirit. God through his Spirit has placed ministries in the church; and since the Spirit is the eschatological Spirit of Joel's prophecy, all of God's people are potential prophets — Jew/Gentile, male/female, home owner/slave. The Spirit is unconscious of race, sex, or rank. He gifts whom he wills for the common good (1 Cor 12:7-11).

Thus the Spirit, as available to all, and gifting various people in diverse ways as he wills, is the crucial ingredient of their new self-understanding — and thus of their discontinuity with the old.

3.3. The Eschatological Framework

The net result of Jesus' death and resurrection followed by the advent of the Spirit was that the early church understood itself to be an eschatological community, "upon whom the end of the ages has come" (1 Cor 10:11). Their citizenship was already in heaven, from whence they were awaiting Christ's return to bring the final consummation (Phil 3:20-21). With the resurrection of Christ God set the future inexorably in motion (1 Cor 15:20-28), so that the form of this present world is passing away (1 Cor 7:31).

Thus the early church understood the future as "already" but "not yet"[30] and its own existence as "between the times." At the Lord's Table they celebrated "the Lord's death until he comes" (1 Cor 11:26). By the resurrection and the gift of the Spirit they had

---

30. Cf. 1 John 3:2: "Beloved, we are God's children *now*, it does *not yet* appear what we shall be, but we know that when he appears we shall be like him, for we shall see him as he is."

139

been stamped with eternity. They had been "born anew to a living hope . . . to an imperishable inheritance preserved in heaven for them" (1 Peter 1:3-5). They already "sat in the heavenlies" through Christ (Eph 1:4). In their present existence, therefore, they were living the life of the future, the way things were eventually to be, as they awaited the consummation. It is thus in light of the eschatological realities of their existence that Paul tries to shame the Corinthians by trivializing both the need to redress one's grievances and the secular courts in which such litigation took place; in light of eschatological realities such things count for nothing (1 Cor 6:1-6).

As much as anything, it is this sense that Christ's death and resurrection marked the turning of the ages, and that the Spirit in/among them was God's down payment and guarantee of their future, that marked the crucial point of discontinuity with what had gone before. With Christ and the Spirit they had *already begun their existence as the future people of God.* And it is precisely this new, eschatological existence that transforms their understanding of being his people. The future has already begun; the Spirit has come upon all of the people alike, so that the only differences between/among them reflect the diversity of the Spirit's gifts, not a hierarchy of persons or offices. There can be no "kings" or "priests" in this new order, precisely because this future kingdom, which was inaugurated by Jesus and the Spirit, is the kingdom *of God,* and thus a return in an even grander way to the theocracy that was God's first order for Israel.

4. STRUCTURE AND MINISTRY IN THE NEW TESTAMENT

As already noted, one of the truly perplexing questions in New Testament studies is to determine the shape that leadership and structures took within the earliest congregations of God's new covenant people. The difficulties here stem from the lack of explicit, intentional instruction, noted at the beginning of this paper. The reasons for it are related both to the twofold reality of their eschatological existence and their experience of the Spirit, not to mention the simple fact that one seldom instructs on something that is generally a given.

What I hope to do here is to offer some reflections on the data as they come to us in the documents. Several things seem quite certain:

4.1. Leadership Was of Two Kinds[31]

On the one hand, there were itinerants, such as the apostle Paul and others, who founded churches and exercised obvious authority over the churches they had founded. On the other hand, when the itinerant founder or his delegate was not present, leadership on the local scene seems to have been left in the hands of "elders,"[32] all expressions of which in the New Testament are plural. Thus Paul founded the church in Corinth, and it is to him that they owe their allegiance — so much so that he rather strongly denounces other "apostles" who teach foreign doctrines on his turf (cf. 2 Cor 10:12-18).

In the same vein Paul delegates Timothy, and apparently later Tychicus, to straighten out the mess in Ephesus created by some false teachers, who in my view were elders who had gone astray.[33] Timothy is not the "pastor"; he is there in Paul's place, exercising Paul's authority. But he is to replace the fallen elders with new ones who will care for the church and teach when Timothy is gone (1 Tim 5:17-22; 2 Tim 2:2; 4:9). The elders in the local churches seem to have been composed of both *episkopoi* (overseers) and *diakonoi* (deacons), who probably had different tasks; but from a distance there is little certainty as to what they were (except that *episkopoi* were to be "capable teachers," 1 Tim 3:2).

Unless Revelation 2–3 provides an exception, there is no evidence in the New Testament of a single leader at the local level who was not at the same time an itinerant. The status of James in Jerusalem is at once a more vexed and complex issue. In an earlier time, as evi-

31. But not of the two kinds most often noted in the literature: charismatic and regular. Rather, it is itinerant and local. Authority lies with the itinerant, whether he is on the local scene or otherwise.

32. Since the earliest congregations grew out of Judaism, the (chiefly lay) elders of the Jewish synagogues almost certainly served as the model for the early Christian communities.

33. See Fee, *1 and 2 Timothy, Titus*, pp. 7-10.

141

denced by both Luke and Paul, he appears to have been one among equals. But as the others moved on and he stayed, he apparently emerged eventually as the predominant leader, but in what capacity one is hard-pressed to determine. In any case, he was not native to Jerusalem — a kind of "permanent itinerant"? — and probably exercised the kind of leadership that Paul did over his churches.

4.2. Apostolic Authority Was Limited

Because of the authority vested in the apostle as founder of churches — either by the apostle himself or as in the case of Epaphras, one of the apostle's co-workers — there does not seem to be any other outside authority for the local churches. That is, apostles apparently did not assume authority in churches they had not founded. Paul's considerably more restrained approach to the church in Rome in contrast to his other letters serves as evidence.

Moreover, even though there is a form of collegiality among the "apostles" and "elders," Paul at least did not consider any one them to have authority over him, although he felt a kind of urgency that they all be in this thing together. Thus, there appears to have been a kind of loose plurality at the top level, with recognition of each other's spheres and ministries as given by God (Gal 2:6-10).

4.3. Not Authority, but Ministry

Apart from the authority of the apostles over the churches they had founded, there seems to be very little interest in the question of "authority" at the local level. To be sure, the people are directed to respect, and submit to, those who labored among them and served them in the Lord (1 Cor 16:16; Heb 13:17). But the interest is not in their authority as such, but in their role as those who care for the others.

The concern for governance and roles within church structures emerges at a *later* time. Nonetheless, the twofold questions of laity and women in ministry are almost always tied to this question in the contemporary evangelical debate. The great urgency always is, Who's in charge around here? which is precisely what puts that debate outside New Testament concerns.

4.4. *Persons, Gifts, and "Office"*

One of the difficulties in the Pauline letters is to determine the relationship between certain gifts, especially prophecy and teaching (in, e.g., 1 Cor 14:6, 26), and people who are designated as prophets and teachers. The clear implication of 1 Cor 14:6 and 26-33 is that teaching, for example, is a gift that might be exercised by anyone in the community; yet in 12:28 he sets prophets and teachers after apostles as God's gifts to the community. Most likely both of these phenomena existed side by side; that is, prophesying and teaching, as well as other gifts, were regularly exercised in a more spontaneous way by any and all within the community, whereas some who exercised these gifts on a regular basis were recognized as "prophets" and "teachers." The former would be ministry for the upbuilding of the community; the latter would naturally emerge in roles of spiritual leadership within the community.

4.5. *Conclusion*

Thus, in the final analysis we know very little about the governance of either the local or larger church. That structures of some kind existed can be taken for granted; but what form these took is simply not an interest in our documents themselves. It is arguable that at least part of the reason for this is their sense of corporate life as the people of God, among whom the leaders themselves did not consider themselves "ordained" to lead the people, but "gifted" to do so as one gift among others.[34]

---

34. In this regard see especially how the participle for leaders "those who care for the church" is found nestled between "contributing to the needs of others" and "showing mercy" in Rom 12:8.

5. SOME HERMENEUTICAL OBSERVATIONS

How, then, does all — or any — of this apply to us? Here our difficulties are a mixture of several realities. First, how does one handle biblical revelation that comes to us less by direct instruction and more by our observations as to what can be gleaned from a whole variety of texts? Second, if we do think in terms of "modeling" after the New Testament church, which of the various models do we opt for, and why? Third, since we are already set in various traditions, and since so much water has gone under the bridge in any case, what difference does any of this make on our very real personal and corporate histories? I have no illusions that I can resolve these matters; indeed, they merely raise some of the deep hermeneutical issues that have long divided the people of God. For most of us, there is comfort in the known, and structures we are used to are easily seen as biblical. Nonetheless, I want to conclude this paper with a few observations.

5.1.

We should probably all yield to the reality that there are no explicitly revealed church structures that serve as the divine order for all times and in all places. Even so, I think there are *ideals* toward which we might strive — although we may very well keep present structures in place. In this regard, I would put at a top level of priority our need to model the church as an eschatological community of the Spirit, in which we think of the church as a whole people among whom leaders serve as one among many other gifts, and that one of the basic priorities of leadership is to equip and enable others for the larger ministry of the church. Despite years of ingrained "division of labor," I am convinced that a more biblical model can be effected within almost any present structure. But it will take a genuine renewal of the Holy Spirit, so that the "clergy" cease being threatened by shared gifts and ministries, and the people cease "paying the preacher to do it."

5.2.

As to structures themselves, it is my guess that the model that emerged was the result of a transference of roles, in which there arose at the local level a more *permanent, single* leader, but now based on the model of the *itinerant apostle*. This bothers me none, as long as the model of a single pastor wielding great authority in the local church is not argued for as something biblical in itself. The danger with this model, of course, is that it tends to focus both authority and ministry in the hands of one or a few persons, who cannot possibly be so gifted as to fill all the needs of the local community. Furthermore, leadership, especially of the more visible kind, can be heady business. For me the great problem with single leadership is its threefold tendency to pride of place, love of authority, and lack of accountability. Whatever else, leadership in the church needs forms that will minimize these tendencies and maximize servanthood.

5.3.

Thus I would urge the movement toward a more biblical view of church and leadership in which we do not eliminate "clergy" — except for all the wrong connotations that that word often brings with it — but look for a renewed leadership and people, in which ordination is not so much to an office as the recognition of the Spirit's prior gifting, and the role of leadership is more often that of Ephesians 4:11-16, preparing the whole church for its ministry to itself and to the world.

5.4.

If the structures of the New Testament church themselves are not necessarily our proper goal, I would urge that the recapturing of the New Testament view of the church itself is. If the church is going to be God's genuine alternative to the world, a people truly for his name, then we must once again become an eschatological people,

people who are citizens of another homeland, whose life in the Spirit is less creedal and cerebral and more fully biblical and experiential, and a people whose sense of corporate existence is so dynamic and genuine that once again it may be said of us, "How those Christians love one another."

Chapter 11

Reflections on Church Order
in the Pastoral Epistles

An old saw says, "Give a dog an ill name and hang him." The same can also be true of a complimentary name. When Paul Anton of Halle (1726) first called Paul's letters to Timothy and Titus the Pastoral Epistles (PE), and it stuck, they have been forever thereafter read and understood as consisting "mostly of advice to younger ministers."[1] However one may feel about the question of authorship,[2] the view as to their occasion and purpose has been basically singular. Whether in Paul's lifetime or later, the letters are seen as responses to

1. See, e.g., A. M. Hunter, *Introducing the New Testament* (2d rev. ed.; London: SCM, 1957), p. 148.
2. Although this is the great problem of the PE and affects nearly everything one says about them, it is much less so for the question of occasion and purpose. For the arguments pro and con for Pauline authorship see (pro) D. Guthrie, *New Testament Introduction* (3d rev. ed.; Downers Grove: InterVarsity, 1970), pp. 584-634; (con) A. T. Hanson, *The Pastoral Epistles* (Grand Rapids: Eerdmans, 1982), pp. 2-51. Although fully aware of the difficulties I am convinced that the PE are ultimately Pauline because, *inter alia,* (1) one can make such good sense of them as fitting the historical situation of the mid-60s; (2) I have yet to have anyone give a good answer to the question: Why three letters? That is, given 1 Timothy, why did a pseudepigrapher write Titus, and given 1 Timothy and Titus and their concerns, why 2 Timothy at all?

the encroachment of alien ideas in some Pauline churches with a view to setting the churches in order as the proper antidote to heresy. Hence they are read and consulted as "church manuals," whose basic intent was to give the ongoing Church instructions on church order in light of Paul's advanced age and impending death (or the decline of his influence at the end of the first century, for those who consider the letters pseudepigraphic). Indeed, so fixed is this view in the Church that I recently taught a course on the exegesis of these letters in a seminary where the students by taking my course could receive credit for their pastoral ministry requirement!

The concerns of this paper are double-edged. First, I want to offer an alternative to the traditional way of viewing the occasion and purpose of the PE (limited to 1 Timothy) and to reexamine the questions of church order in light of that purpose. Second, I hope to reopen the hermeneutical questions about church order in light of this exegesis and offer some suggestions about contemporary relevance. These are suggestions at best; no specific applications to any local church or denomination are being contended for.

The "church manual" approach to the PE has almost always paid lip-service to the threat of the false teachers (FT) as the occasion of 1 Timothy but has usually all but lost sight of that occasion when exegeting the letter, except for the places where the FT are specifically mentioned. Thus after setting the stage in chap. 1 by ordering Timothy to stop the FT, Paul's real concern, the "ordering" of the church, begins in chap. 2 with instructions on prayer (2:1-8). This in turn gives way to a discussion on the role of women in the church — they are to be quiet (2:9-15) — which is followed by instructions for the appointment of overseers and deacons (3:1-13). After another brief note about the FT in 4:1-5, Paul sets Timothy forth as a model for ministry (4:6–5:2). In chap. 5 he sets out the qualifications for a ministering order of widows (5:3-16) and rules for the pay and discipline of elders (5:17-25). He concludes in chap. 6 by returning to the theme of the FT (6:3-5) and of Timothy's serving as a pastoral model of perseverance and holding fast the truth of the gospel.

As popular and deeply entrenched as that view is — on both sides of the question of authenticity — there are several reasons for doubting it as an accurate reflection of what is happening in 1 Timothy.

Besides the rather total lack of logic to the argument of the letter as thus presented, one must ruefully admit that we are left with far more questions about church order than answers. (Surely this whole perspective should have been questioned long ago simply on the existential grounds that such diverse groups as Roman Catholics, Plymouth Brethren, and Presbyterians all use the PE to support their ecclesiastical structures.)

Furthermore a careful exegesis of the whole, as well as of most of the individual paragraphs, of 1 Timothy suggests that this view has enormous exegetical difficulties to overcome. For example, any careful reading of 2:1-7 reveals that the concern in this paragraph is not with instruction on prayer as such, nor on the necessity of four kinds of prayer being offered in church, nor on prayer for rulers so that believers can live peaceable lives (the most common views). Rather, the emphasis is that prayer be made for all people, precisely because this is pleasing to the one God who wants all people to be saved, and for the sake of whom Christ is the one mediator, having given himself a ransom for all people. That emphasis scarcely accords with the "church manual" approach to the paragraph and is therefore commonly slighted or neglected altogether.

If 1 Timothy is not primarily a church manual, what then? The key to its purpose, as proposed here, is to take with full seriousness three pieces of data: Paul's own statements of purpose in 1 Tim 1:3 and 3:15 and the content of Paul's farewell address as given by Luke in Acts 20:17-35, especially 20:30.

(1) In 1 Tim 1:3 Paul explicitly tells Timothy that the reason he was left in Ephesus was not to set the church in order (cf. Titus 1:5) but to "command certain [people] not to teach false doctrines any longer" (NIV). The whole of 1 Timothy in fact is dominated by this singular concern, and it is clear from the letter that their teaching involves both doctrinal and behavioral aberrations. Based on speculations about the OT (= myths and wearisome genealogies, 1:4; cf. 1:7; Titus 1:14-16; 3:9), this false teaching is being presented as *gnōsis* (6:20) and apparently has an esoteric — and exclusivistic — appeal.[3]

---

3. The question of the nature of the false teaching is not fully agreed upon. The term "Gnostic," especially in its second-century form, is rather thoroughly mislead-

This exclusivism is furthered by an appeal to an ascetic ideal (4:3; perhaps 5:23; cf. Titus 1:14-16), which in Titus 1:14 is caricatured in the language of Isa 29:13 as "the commandments of men." The FT themselves made their teachings a matter of quarreling and strife, battling over mere words, Paul says (6:3-5). Indeed, over against the "healthy teaching" of the gospel they have a "sickly craving" for controversy,[4] and the bottom line is greed. They have come to view their religious instruction as a means of turning a drachma (6:5-10; cf 3:3, 8). For Paul such teaching is ultimately demonic (4:1-2), and those who have followed it have gone astray after Satan (5:15; cf. 2:14; 3:6-7; 2 Tim 2:25).

Unfortunately, many seem to be capitulating (4:1; 6:21; cf. 2 Tim 1:15; 2:18; 4:3-4), and that is the great urgency of this letter — for Timothy to stop the FT and thereby, by his own example and teaching, to save his hearers (4:16).

(2) Thus the point of his second statement as to the reason for writing (3:15) is not so "that thou mayest know how thou oughtest to behave thyself in the house of God" (KJV), implying that Timothy would hereby learn how to do things "in church," but so that "you will know what kind of conduct befits a member of God's household" (NAB).[5] That is, Paul is giving instructions on how God's true

---

ing. Few of the essential ingredients of that system are present. I am inclined to a view that sees genuine affinities with the "heresy" in Colosse a few years earlier, which is probably a form of Hellenistic Judaism that has imbibed a good deal from Hellenism. For earlier but divergent forms of this view see J. B. Lightfoot, *Biblical Essays* (London: Macmillan, 1893), pp. 411-18; F. J. A. Hort, *Judaistic Christianity* (London: Macmillan, 1894), pp. 132-33.

4. For the use of medical imagery ("sound" or "healthy" teaching; "sickly craving for controversy") in polemical contexts in Hellenism and the PE see A. J. Malherbe, "Medical Imagery in the Pastoral Epistles," in *Texts and Testaments: Critical Essays on the Bible and Early Church Fathers,* ed. W. E. March (San Antonio: Trinity University, 1980), pp. 19-35.

5. There is no expressed subject of the infinitive *anastrephesthai* ("to conduct oneself") in Paul's sentence, and it must be inferred from the context. The KJV's "thou . . . thyself" is the least likely option. The GNB has "we . . . ourselves," but "people . . . themselves" (NAB, NIV, NEB) is to be preferred. The Living Bible's "you will know what kind of men you choose as officers of the church" is altogether unwarranted.

people ought to behave, and it is not like the FT. Indeed, the whole of chaps. 2–3 is best understood as instruction vis-à-vis the behavior and attitudes of the FT.[6]

(3) When one adds the evidence from Acts 20:30, it is clear that Timothy's task in Ephesus, in contrast to Titus's on Crete, is not that of appointing elders. The church in Ephesus already had elders several years earlier, and Paul in this speech is predicting that from among their own number will arise those who will lead the church astray.[7] Take the content of that prediction seriously as actually having come to pass and the whole of 1 Timothy falls into place. The reason for the great urgency in 1 Timothy, and for Paul's concern over Timothy's own reception and well-being, lies in the probability that the FT in that letter were some elders who had themselves strayed from Paul's gospel and were in the process of taking the church, or many within the church, with them into error.

This probability is supported by several other data:

(a) Quite in contrast to Galatians or 2 Corinthians, there is not a hint in 1 or 2 Timothy that the FT are outsiders. In fact everything points to their being insiders.[8] They clearly function as teachers (1:3; 6:7; 6:3); they have themselves wandered away from and made shipwreck of their faith (1:6, 19); and two of them are named and have been excommunicated (1:20).

Since teaching is the one clearly expressed duty of the elders (3:3; 5:17), it follows naturally that the FT were already teachers — thus elders — who have gone astray.

(b) It seems certain from 2:9-15; 5:11-15; 2 Tim 3:6-7 that the FT

---

6. The full presentation of this position may be found in my commentary on the PE in the New International Biblical Commentary series (Hendrickson, 1988).

7. The data of this speech need to be taken more seriously by scholars on both sides of the question of authenticity. If it is true prediction, then Luke's recording of it accords with what he knows to have taken place. If the speech was created by Luke *after* the fact, then it is best argued that he really did so after *the fact* — that is, he based it on what he knew to have happened in Ephesus. In either case the defection of some Ephesian elders in the 60s looks like a piece of solid historical datum.

8. The only other person I know to have articulated this position is E. E. Ellis, "Paul and His Opponents," in *Prophecy and Hermeneutic in Early Christianity* (Grand Rapids: Eerdmans, 1978), p. 114. He does not, however, pursue its implications for the occasion and purpose of the letter.

THE TEXT AND THE LIFE OF THE CHURCH

have had considerable influence among some women, especially some younger widows. These women have opened their homes to the FT and have themselves become the propagators of the new teachings. In 5:13 they are described as busybodies, speakers of foolishness, going from house to house[9] and saying things they should not (cf. the similar description of the FT in 1:6-7); and in v. 15 they are declared to have "already turned away to follow Satan." Since in 2 Tim 3:6-7 the FT, depicted now as religious charlatans like the Egyptian magicians who opposed Moses, worm their way into the homes of these women, it is highly likely that the women are themselves well maintained and are the source of the FT's "dishonest gain." This also explains the great concern of 5:3-16, which is not to set up an order of ministering widows[10] but to distinguish those "genuine" (*ontōs;* 5:3, 5, 16) widows, who need to be supported by the church, from these younger widows who are part of the trouble in Ephesus.[11]

(c) It is therefore altogether likely, based both on the evidence of 2 Tim 3:6-7 (the FT making their way into houses) and of 1 Cor 16:19 (Aquila and Priscilla have a "house church" in Ephesus), that corporate life in the church in Ephesus was not experienced in a large Sunday gathering in a single sanctuary but in many house churches, each with its own elder(s). If so, then 2:8 is a word for each of these house churches: "I want the men in every place (*en panti topō*

---

9. To translate *phlyaroi* "gossips," as is done in most English translations, is both misleading and prejudicial. The word means to "talk foolishness" but not in the sense that "gossip" connotes. Rather, in most of its extant uses it means to prate on about something, either in a foolish manner or with foolish ideas. In the latter sense it is picked up in polemical contexts to refer to speaking what is foolish or absurd vis-à-vis the truth — precisely Paul's condemnation of the FT in 1:6; 6:20; 2 Tim 2:23.

10. This is a frequently maintained position, based on some second-century texts (see, e.g., J. N. D. Kelly, *A Commentary on the Pastoral Epistles* [New York: Harper, 1963], p. 112). But those texts are not at all clear that a "ministering order" existed. Rather, they allude to their existence as a recognizable group and reflect concern for their care.

11. Thus vv. 3-8 set up two criteria: (1) They must be without family to support them; (2) they must be godly in their own right, noted for the good works mentioned in v. 10.

152

= in every place where believers gather in and around Ephesus)[12] to pray (= while in the gathered assembly), lifting up holy hands (the natural posture for prayer)[13] without anger or disputing (i.e., unlike the FT who are doing precisely that)." Paul's point is that he wants the various gatherings (= house churches) of God's people in Ephesus to be for prayer (= worship), not places for carrying on the speculations and controversies of the FT.

What one can envision, therefore, on the basis of all this evidence is a scene in which the various house churches each had one or more elders. The issue therefore was not so much that a large gathered assembly was being split down the middle as that various house churches were capitulating almost altogether to its leadership that had gone astray. Some new ideas that had been circulating in the Lycus valley (Colosse, Laodicea) just a few years earlier[14] had made their way to Ephesus, but now as the "official" line being promulgated by some of its elders. They must be stopped, and Timothy was left in Ephesus to do it.

The purpose of 1 Timothy, then, arises out of these complexities. The letter betrays evidences everywhere that it was intended for the church itself, not just Timothy. But because of defections in the leadership Paul does not, as before, write directly to the church but to the church through Timothy. The reason for going this route would have been twofold: (1) to encourage Timothy himself to carry out this most difficult task of stopping the erring elders, who had become thoroughly disputatious, and (2) to authorize Timothy before the church to carry out his task. At the same time, of course, the church will be having the false teachers/teachings exposed before them. Thus 1 Timothy lacks the standard thanksgiving (cf. the more personal 2 Tim 1:3-5) and the personal greetings at the end,

12. This prepositional phrase could mean "everywhere" (as NIV), but when Paul intends that he usually says it (1 Cor 11:26; 14:33). Furthermore to universalize the prepositional phrase when the rest of the sentence so clearly fits the specific situation in Ephesus makes little sense.

13. For references to prayer with uplifted hands in Judaism see *inter alia* 1 Kgs 8:54; Pss 63:4; 141:2; 2 Macc 14:32; Philo *Flaccus* 121; Josephus *Ant.* 4:40; for early Christianity see esp. Tertullian *On Prayer* 17.

14. See n. 3 above.

and such personal words to Timothy as do appear (e.g., 1:18-19; 4:6-16; 6:11-14) are totally subservient to his task to restore order to the church.

Such an occasion and purpose also helps to explain another phenomenon of the letter — viz., that Paul is forever calling on Timothy to teach "sound" or "healthy" doctrine, but without spelling out the nature or content of such teaching.[15] The reason is now obvious. The letter was written to a lifelong companion, who would not have needed such instruction. But the church had to hear that the deviations were a disease among them and that what Timothy would have to teach would be the words of health (cf. 1:10). Just as in 1 Cor 4:17, Timothy was there to remind the church of Paul's ways. The letter that would so authorize him would not at the same time need a detailing of those "ways."

What is needed at this point is to trace the argument of the whole of 1 Timothy to show how it functions as a response to this proposed historical reconstruction. But that would take us in a different direction and is available in my recent commentary.[16] Our concern here is to examine what is said about church order in this letter in light of this understanding of the occasion and purpose of the letter.

First, it must be noted again that 1 Timothy is not intended to establish church order but to respond in a very *ad hoc* way to the Ephesian situation with its straying elders. To put that in another way: What we learn about church order in 1 Timothy is not so much organizational as reformational. We see reflections of church structures, not organizational charts; paradigms, not imperatives; qualifications, not duties; the correcting of error and abuses, not a "how to" manual on church organization. Reconstructing church order from this epistle, therefore, falls into the same category of difficulty as the attempt to reconstruct an early Christian gathering for worship on the basis of 1 Corinthians 11–14.

---

15. This is a common objection to Pauline authorship; see, e.g., how R. J. Karris begins his article, "The Background and Significance of the Polemic of the Pastoral Episitles," *JBL* 92 (1973): 549-64.

16. See n. 6 above.

Thus the church already had elders (1 Tim 5:17), but some of them were persisting in sin and needed to be publicly exposed or rebuked (5:20) so that others would take warning.[17] Their replacements must be proven people (5:22, 24-25; 3:4-7, 10) who have a reputation for exemplary ("blameless," 3:2, 8) behavior that in every way stands in sharp contrast to the FT. The latter forbid marriage (4:3); true elders are to be exemplary husbands and fathers (3:2, 4-5, 12).[18] The FT think "godliness is a means to financial gain" (6:5); true elders must not be lovers of money (3:3, 8). The FT are quarrelsome and divisive (6:4-5); true elders must be "not violent but gentle, not quarrelsome" (3:3).

Likewise with the women. It may be assumed that women functioned as proclaimers of the gospel in Ephesus, just as in other Pauline churches (1 Cor 11:4-5; Rom 16:1; Phil 4:3; cf. Priscilla in Acts). But because the young widows who are party to the FT have had a disruptive effect on this church (5:13, 15), the women are instructed to dress modestly (2:9-10; in contrast to those who have become wanton, 5:11-12), to learn in quietness (2:11-12; in contrast to those who go about from house [church?] to house saying things about which they know nothing, 5:13), and finally to marry and raise a family (2:15; 5:14), as any decent, "godly" woman in that culture should do.

However, to say that what we learn is not intentionally organizational but corrective does not mean that we cannot learn from that correction. My point is that such "instruction," as almost always in Paul, is not intentionally systematic but incidental and occasional, and we must be careful in our systematizing not to overlook the occasional nature of the material as it comes to us. What, then, may we say with a high degree of certainty about church order from the PE?

17. This assumes, with Kelly *(Commentary)*, J. P. Meier, *("Presbyteros* in the Pastoral Epistles," *CBQ* [1973]: 325-37), and others that all of 5:17-25 is dealing with the discipline and replacement of elders, against Lock *(Commentary,* ICC), Dibelius-Conzelmann *(Commentary,* Hermeneia), and others who think vv. 20-25 have to do with the restoration of penitent sinners.

18. It is tempting, on the basis of 2:9-10; 3:2; 5:11-15; 2 Tim 3:6-7 and the reminders to Timothy that he must keep himself pure (1 Tim 5:2, 22), to see a sexual liaison between the FT and the younger widows. But the suggestion is somewhat speculative.

(1) It is a mistaken notion to view Timothy or Titus as model pastors for a local church. The letters simply have no such intent. Although it is true that Timothy and Titus carry full apostolic authority, in both cases they are itinerants on special assignment who are there as Paul's apostolic delegates, not as permanent resident pastors. This is a far cry from Timothy's role in Ephesus, and Titus's in the churches of Crete, and that of Ignatius in Antioch or Polycarp in Smyrna fifty years later.

Timothy, it is true, is called upon to set an example for Christian behavior (4:12), but this is exactly the role Paul had in his churches. They were to learn the "ways" of Christ by following the apostolic model (2 Thess 1:6; 2:14; 1 Cor 4:16; 11:1). Both Timothy and Titus are expected to teach, exhort, and rebuke, of course, which would also be the function of the elders after Paul and his itinerant co-workers had left. But these were first of all apostolic functions.

(2) Responsibility for leadership in local churches (per town or, as is likely in larger cities like Ephesus, per house church) was from the beginning in the hands of several people, who apparently had been appointed by the apostle and his co-workers (cf. Acts 14:23). In the earliest letters these people are styled *hoi proistamenoi* (1 Thess 5:12; Rom 12:8), language still being used at the time of the PE (1 Tim 3:5; 5:17). Interestingly, however, despite all the difficulties in some of these churches, none of the letters is ever addressed to these people, nor are they ever given charge to set the church in order or withstand error. In Phil 1:1 Paul for the first time addresses both the church and its (plural) leaders (*episkopoi*, "overseers," and *diakonoi*, "deacons," the identical words used in 1 Tim 3:2, 8; cf. Titus 1:7). Apart from this reference we would not have otherwise known of their earlier existence. But because of such a reference we may properly assume that other churches also had such plural leadership. It should be finally noted that in none of the earlier letters does the term "elder" *(presbyteros)* appear.

The evidence that emerges in the PE corresponds very closely to this state of affairs. Although some have argued that Timothy and Titus were to appoint a single *episkopos* under whom there would be a group of deacons, exegesis of the key passages (1 Tim 3:1-2, 8; 5:17; Titus 1:5-7) and a comparison with Acts 20:17, 28 indicates otherwise.

156

In all cases leadership was plural. These leaders are called elders in 1 Tim 5:17; Titus 1:5. They were to be appointed in Crete by Titus but had been appointed some years earlier in Ephesus, probably by Paul himself. The term "elders" is probably a covering term for both overseers and deacons. In any case the grammar of Titus 1:5, 7 demands that "elder" and "overseer" are interchangeable terms (as in Acts 20:17, 28), but they are not thereby necessarily coextensive.[19]

(3) What were the duties of such elders? At this point our information is limited, precisely because this was not Paul's concern. Two things seem certain: (a) The elders called overseers were responsible for teaching (1 Tim 3:3; 5:17; Titus 1:9), for which they were to receive remuneration (1 Tim 5:17);[20] (b) the elders together were responsible for "managing" or "caring for" the local church (see 1 Tim 3:4-5; 5:17), whatever that might have involved at that time in its history. Beyond that, everything is speculative.

(4) But we do learn something about their qualifications for appointment (or in 1 Timothy perhaps the "yardstick" against which existing elders were to be measured). They must not be new converts (3:6; 5:22). Indeed Paul has been burned badly enough by the present defecting elders that Timothy is to exercise great patience in appointing their replacements (vv. 24-25). Above all they must be exemplary family men, which is what the difficult "husband of one wife" (3:2, 12; Titus 1:6) must at least mean, although it also is very likely a frowning upon second marriages of any kind.[21] The reason

---

19. For an excellent discussion of these matters see R. E. Brown, "*Episcopē* and *Episkopos:* The New Testament Evidence," *TS* 41 (1980): 322-38.

20. The phrase "double honor" almost certainly means "the same honor afforded others, plus a stipend."

21. This is one of the truly difficult phrases in the PE (cf. 5:9 of the "true" widows; Titus 1:6). There are at least four options: (1) It is required that the overseer be married. Support is found in the fact that the false teachers are forbidding marriage and that Paul urges marriage for the wayward widows (5:14; cf. 2:15). But against it is (a) it emphasizes "wife," while the text emphasizes "one"; (b) the fact that Paul and most likely Timothy were not married; (c) it stands in contradiction to 1 Cor 7:25-38. Besides, it was a cultural presupposition that most people would be married. (2) It prohibits polygamy. This correctly emphasizes the "one wife" aspect, but polygamy was such a rare feature of pagan society that such a prohibition would function as a near irrelevancy. Moreover, it would not seem to fit the identical phrase used of the wid-

for this emphasis is twofold: (a) It stands as the antithesis to the FT; (b) such people who do their "home work" well in the basic Christian community, the family, have already qualified themselves for God's extended family, the church.

When such leaders sin or go astray they are to be disciplined. No unsupported charge may be brought against anyone (5:19), but there must be public rebuke of those who persist (5:20).

(5) It is not at all clear that there were "orders" of women's ministries, including widows. In the commentary I argue that there were women who served the church in some capacity, perhaps including leadership (1 Tim 3:11), but that there was no order of widows, who were enrolled and had prescribed duties.[22]

(6) What seems certain in all of this is that the church order of the PE fits easily with what one finds in the other Pauline letters and Acts. Contrariwise it is unlike the Ignatian epistles both in spirit and in details. This in turn is an argument for their authenticity, not against it.

Thus we do not learn nearly as much as we should have liked. But we do learn quite a bit. The question before us now is how what

---

ows in 5:9. (3) It prohibits second marriages (RSV, "married only once"). Such an interpretation is supported by many of the data: (a) It would fit the widow especially; (b) all kinds of inscriptional evidence praises women (especially, although sometimes men) who were "married only once" and remained "faithful" to that marriage after one's partner had died. (See M. Lightman and W. Ziesel, "Univera: An Example of Continuity and Change in Roman Society," *CH* 46 [1977]: 19-32.) This view would then prohibit second marriages after death, but it would also obviously — perhaps especially — prohibit divorce and remarriage. Some scholars (e.g., Hanson) would make it refer only to the latter. (4) It requires marital fidelity to one wife (cf. NEB: "faithful to his one wife"; see C. H. Dodd, "New Testament Translation Problems II," *BibTr* 28 [1977]: 112-16). In this view the church leader is required to live an exemplary life (marriage is assumed), faithful to his one wife in a culture where marital infidelity was common and at times assumed. It would of course also rule out polygamy and divorce and remarriage, but it would not necessarily rule out the remarriage of a widower (although that would still not be the Pauline ideal; cf. 1 Cor 7:8-9, 39-40). Although there is much to be said for either understanding of option 3, the concern that the Church's leaders live exemplary married lives seems best to fit the context — given the apparently low view of marriage and family on the part of the false teachers (4:3).

22. Although there is a genuine concern for the care of "true" widows — i.e., those without children — the great urgency of 5:3-16 is with the younger widows who had "gone astray after Satan."

we learn, as over against what we are specifically taught or commanded, functions as God's Word for us.

The matter of the relevance of these conclusions to the present scene is at once more pressing and more problematic — and requires another full-length paper far beyond the limitations of this one. Part of the difficulty, of course, stems from the fractured nature of the twentieth-century Church. But part of it is also due to inconsistent or assumed hermeneutics at a much deeper level than the mere application or nonapplication of a given text to a given situation. My present concerns lie with these deeper levels, which can only be lightly touched on here.

(1) At the heart of the question of church order, more than for many issues, is the prior question of the role of tradition (or Church) in interpretation. At issue is the whole question of authority structures and how one understands "apostolic succession," especially so for Protestants of a more congregational or presbyterial church order.

For Roman Catholicism this issue has long ago been resolved. The apostolic succession, meaning the authority of the apostles, resides with the clergy and is represented at the local level by the parish priest. Most Protestants, chiefly because of what they see as abuses of the use of tradition (which is seen at times not simply to interpret Scripture, or to provide help where Scripture is silent, but actually to contravene Scripture), reject the apostolic succession as having to do with persons or structures and see it as resting in the truth of the gospel itself. Although it is seldom put this way, the NT functions for Protestants as the apostolic succession.

But such a view also has its inherent weaknesses — and abuses. For example, although most Protestants in theory deny apostolic succession to reside in its clergy, *de facto* it is practiced in vigorous and sometimes devastating ways — in the "one-man show" of many denominational churches or in the little dictatorships in other (especially "independent") churches. And how did such a pluralism of papacies emerge? Basically from two sources (not to mention the fallenness of the clergy whose egos often love such power): (a) from the fact that the local pastor is so often seen (and often sees him/herself) as the authoritative interpreter of the "sole authority" — Scripture; (b) from

159

the pastor's functioning in the role of authority, thus assuming the mantle of Paul or of a Timothy or Titus. Hence it is based strictly on the use of a paradigm, the validity of which is scarcely ever questioned. Here Protestant "tradition" has the final say.

But on what hermeneutical grounds does one justify the use of this paradigm? Why not the real paradigm of 1 Timothy — plural leadership at the local level? Or, to put this whole question at a different hermeneutical level altogether, if the NT is one's "sole authority" and that authority does not in fact teach anything directly about church order at the local level, then one might rightly ask whether there is a normative church order. If the best one has is paradigms, then it is certainly arguable that whatever paradigm one goes with it should minimize the potentiality of individual overlordship or authoritarianism and maximize accountability and servanthood.

(2) The other hermeneutical difficulty, related in part to the previous one, has to do with the application or nonapplication of specific texts. In its basic form the question is this: How do these *ad hoc* documents, inspired of the Spirit to address and correct a singular historical situation, function by that same Spirit as eternal Word for us? As I have pointed out elsewhere, the great problem here is with consistency; and even though common sense keeps us from going too far afield, our individual "common sense" is not always common, since it is informed by diverse cultural, theological, and ecclesiastical traditions.[23]

In light of the earlier conclusions about church order in 1 Timothy, this hermeneutical question might be rephrased: How does what we learn from a text that is not intended specifically to teach church order function for us today? Or to put it even more specifically: Do imperatives directed toward the church in Ephesus in A.D. 62, to correct abuses of wayward elders, function as eternal norms, obligatory in every culture in every age in an absolute way?

The problem here is twofold: (a) our own inconsistencies; (b) difficulties created by exegetical ambiguity. For example: (1) A consid-

<hr/>

23. See G. Fee and D. Stuart, *How to Read the Bible for All Its Worth* (Grand Rapids: Zondervan, 1982), pp. 37-71.

erable literature has emerged over 1 Tim 2:11-12, pro and con, as to whether women may teach, preach, or be ordained. But there is not a single piece that argues from 5:3-16 that the church should care for its over-sixty widows or require the younger ones to be married. One can understand the reasons for this, of course. Our agendas have been set by our own cultural or existential urgencies. But the inconsistency is there. To get those who are doing battle over 2:11-12 to own up to it is extremely difficult. (2) Both of these texts can also serve to illustrate the problem of exegetical ambiguity. So also with the requirement in 3:2, 12 that the church leader be "the husband of one wife." How, for example, can one deny ministry to people who were divorced and remarried before becoming believers, on the basis of this text, yet allow former adulterers to serve, who may have lived with several women, without legally marrying them, and not even take into consideration that in this case the text also probably prohibits remarriage of widow/widowers? The very exegetical ambiguity or uncertainty needs hermeneutical discussion — that is, how does it apply if we cannot even be sure of what it means?

Another form of this ambiguity is related to the reality of Scripture's broader witness in some cases. For example, Paul's words in 2:11-12 or 5:14 must be wrestled with respectively in light of Phil 4:3 or 1 Cor 7:8-9, 39-40, for example. The very differences reflected in these texts point to their *ad hoc* nature, which probably in turn argues for more flexibility and less rigidity than one sometimes finds in the literature.

Back, then, to our question. Do such texts have a kind of absolute normativeness? If so, how so? And what do we do with the magnitude of our disobedience to those texts that are not urgent to us?

I would argue that the answer lies in the area of our obedience to the point of the text, its "spirit" if you will, even if at times the specifics are not followed to the "letter." This is how all of us treat 1 Tim 6:1-2 — although such was not always the case.[24] This is prob-

---

24. The arguments of J. H. Hopkins, A. T. Bledsoe, T. Stringfellow, and C. B. Hodge, among others, for a biblical base for slavery are remarkably — and frighteningly — similar to those who oppose women's ordination; see especially W. M. Swartley, *Slavery, Sabbath, War and Women* (Scottdale, PA: Herald, 1983).

ably how many would argue that they are obeying 5:3-16 — although I for one would like to probe a bit more here. Why not, then, with 2:11-12, since all do it with the preceding vv. 9-10?

Let me say finally to those who see the raising of questions this way as a ploy to get around something: Such is not the case. My hermeneutical concern is quite the opposite: obedience. But I also want greater hermeneutical consistency. We who take Scripture seriously as Word of God must stop our "pick and choose" approach to obedience, or at least articulate reasons for it.

Chapter 12

The Kingdom of God
and the Church's Global Mission

T he thesis of this chapter is that the roots of our conviction about the global mission of the church are to be found in Jesus' proclamation of the kingdom of God[1] — as already present in his own mission and message. For those who know that message well, this global implication may come as something of a surprise, since not much of his explicit teaching would appear to lead to that conclusion.[2] Although the evangelists themselves clearly see the Gentile, thus "global," implications of Jesus' ministry,[3] and even though

---

1. Although this is not the place to argue for it, I am equally convinced that all of the key issues in NT theology have their roots ultimately in the mission and message of Jesus (the focus on Jesus as Messiah and Son of God, who through his death and resurrection effected salvation for God's new people, who constitute an eschatological community of disciples, living in the present by the Spirit as they await the final consummation of that salvation).

2. For an overview of this material and its significance for our subject, see Ferdinand Hahn, *Mission in the New Testament*, Studies in Biblical Theology 47 (London: SCM, 1965), pp. 26-46.

3. In Mark's Gospel this recognition is found, for example, in his inclusion of people from "the regions across the Jordan and around Tyre and Sidon," who joined the large crowds that came to hear him (3:8); for this perspective see further 5:1-20; 6:53-56; 7:24-37, plus the quotation of Isa 56:7 that the temple shall be a

some of his activities[4] and sayings[5] include an openness toward Samaritans and Gentiles, Jesus' own ministry was directed primarily to "the lost sheep of the house of Israel" (Matt 15:24).[6] Nonetheless, I hope herewith to demonstrate (1) that the global mission of the church rests ultimately in Jesus' proclamation of the "good news of the kingdom," especially as good news to "the poor"; and (2) that such a proclamation is to be understood as the fulfillment of the covenant with Abraham, embraced by the prophetic tradition, that God's intent from the beginning has been to bless "all the peoples on earth" (Gen 12:3).

---

house of prayer for all nations, and especially 13:10: "The gospel must first be preached to all nations." In Luke's Gospel, interestingly enough, even though Jesus is announced at the beginning as the one who was to be "a light for revelation to the Gentiles" (2:32), and after his resurrection he commissions his disciples to go to the "ends of the earth" (Acts 1:8), the actual Gentile mission itself belongs more to the period of the Spirit in the church than it does to the earthly ministry of Jesus (although he does include some of the "Q" sayings material that has a Gentile perspective). Although Matthew perceives Jesus' ministry as more strictly to Israel, he also anticipates the Gentile mission in such passages as 4:15; 8:11; 10:16; 12:18; 21:43; and 24:14. The mission of the church to the nations is made specific in the Great Commission in 28:19.

4. The narrative in John 4, the story of the grateful Samaritan (Luke 17:12-19), and the parable of the so-called Good Samaritan (Luke 10:30-37) indicate at least an attempt on the part of Jesus to build bridges toward the Samaritans; likewise the narratives of the centurion of Capernaum (Matt 8:5-10, 13 = Luke 7:1-9) and of the Syro-Phoenician woman (Mark 7:24-30 par.) indicate a readiness to cross the boundaries on behalf of Gentiles.

5. Especially Matt 8:11-12 (= Luke 13:28-29), which is generally conceded by most scholars as authentic, and which seems to function as a prophetic judgment against Israel — with a view to the gathering of Gentiles. Hahn, *Mission*, 34, would also include in this category the judgment against the cities in Matt 11:21 (= Luke 10:13-15), in which greater hope is given to the cities judged by the OT prophets (Tyre and Sidon) than for the cities of Galilee. Although many would deny their authenticity, we must also include here the saying in Mark 13:10 (= Matt 24:14; the gospel to the Gentiles) and the Great Commission in Matt 28:16-20.

6. Cf. the mission instructions to the Twelve in Matt 10:6.

AN OUTLINE OF JESUS' PROCLAMATION
OF THE KINGDOM[7]

The universal witness of the Synoptic tradition is that the absolutely central theme of Jesus' mission and message was "the good news of the kingdom of God." This claim can be demonstrated in a number of ways.

1. Whenever the evangelists themselves summarize the mission of Jesus, they invariably do so in terms of the kingdom of God. This is true not only of Mark's opening summary of Jesus' proclamation (1:15: "The time is fulfilled; the kingdom of God is at hand; repent and believe the good news"), but also of all such summaries in the Synoptic Gospels.[8]

2. When Jesus sends out first the Twelve (Matt 10:7) and then the Seventy-two (Luke 10:9),[9] the only specific instruction given in both instances is: "As you go, preach this message, 'The kingdom of heaven is near.'"

3. It is always on his own lips. Such language is sparse in the remaining literature of contemporary Judaism; it is relatively infrequent in the rest of the NT.[10] Yet it is the predominant note in the teaching of Jesus,[11] including at least eighteen different expressions found only in that teaching and nowhere else in all of Jewish or Christian literature (e.g., "to seize the kingdom," "to enter the king-

---

7. For more complete presentations of this theme in Jesus, with full argumentation and documentation, see especially Joachim Jeremias, *New Testament Theology: The Proclamation of Jesus* (New York: Charles Scribner's Sons, ET 1971), and George Eldon Ladd, *The Presence of the Future: The Eschatology of Biblical Realism*, rev. ed. (Grand Rapids: Eerdmans, 1974).

8. See, e.g., the nearly identical summaries at the beginning of the first two major sections of Matthew's Gospel (4:23; 9:35); cf. Luke 8:1 (and also his addition in 4:43 to Mark 1:38: "I must preach *the good news of the kingdom of God* to the other towns also").

9. For the argument that the original text here is "seventy-two" rather than "seventy," see B. M. Metzger, *A Textual Commentary on the Greek New Testament* (New York: United Bible Societies, 1971), pp. 150-51.

10. In the Gospel of John 3 times; Paul, 10; Acts, 8; Hebrews, 1; James, 1; the Revelation, 2.

11. It appears 49 times in Matthew, 15 in Mark, and 41 in Luke.

dom," "to seek the kingdom," "the mystery of the kingdom," "the keys of the kingdom," "the least/greatest in the kingdom").[12]

Thus, it is fair to say that to miss — or to misunderstand — this term is to miss Jesus altogether. The question is, What does it mean? As a convenient way to outline what Jesus was all about, we are well served by Mark's little summary (1:14-15).

The Time Is Fulfilled

These first words of the summary suggest two related realities about Jesus' understanding of the kingdom. First, the kingdom of God is an *eschatological* term, belonging primarily to the category of "time" rather than "space." It refers to a time that was *promised* and was to be *fulfilled,* not to a place where people were to go. Thus, reflecting several kinds of themes from the OT,[13] the kingdom of God refers primarily to the time of the future — the Eschaton ("End") — when God would finally excercise his kingly rule over the whole of his created order. Those around Jesus, therefore, never ask about *what* or *where,* but "*when* does it come?"[14] They are looking for the time in the future when God will "wrap it up" as far as the present is concerned.

Second, and closely related, the language of "fulfillment" indicates that the kingdom of God is ultimately tied to *Jewish messianic* (= end-time) *expectations.* These go back as far as the covenant made with Abraham, that through his seed "all the peoples on earth will be blessed" (Gen 12:3). They found historical focus in the throne of David, so that in the ensuing years both people and prophet looked back longingly to David's time and yearned for the days of former glory. This hope is reflected especially in such Psalms as 2 and 72,

---

12. Cf. Jeremias, *New Testament Theology,* 32-34.

13. The idea goes back nearly to the beginning of Israel's own history that God was its only king; and even when its people were given a king, he was understood to be an earthly representative of the divine kingship. Thus, God's kingship is frequently celebrated in the Psalms, as well as presupposed in many of the prophetic oracles.

14. See especially Luke 17:20-21; cf. 19:11.

which were probably originally composed for the coronation of the Davidic kings, but in time came to be understood as pointing to the "great king" of the future.

As the prophets in particular gave articulation to this hope, they saw the future in terms of judgment and salvation — judgment not only on the surrounding nations, but especially on Israel, because it had failed to keep covenant with its God, Yahweh. Instead of worshiping and serving Yahweh alone, and doing his will, expressed in the covenant stipulations of the law, the people of Israel gave themselves to every kind of idolatry, sexual immorality, and injustice. Thus, the day of the Lord, the great day of the future, would be "a day of darkness and gloom, a day of clouds and blackness" (Joel 2:2; cf. Amos 5:18-20); included would be an overthrow of the oppressor, the idolator, the adulterer. The old values would be overturned; God would come with justice and judge all those who had not walked in his ways.

But because it was "Yahweh's day," it would also be a day of salvation for that righteous remnant who were doing his will, as well as for those who, chastised by the judgment, would return to the Lord. Because it would be God's day, his supreme day, the whole creation would feel the effects of his redemption: the vine would produce in abundance (Amos 9:13); the cow would feed with the bear, and their young lie down together (Isa 11:7). Especially — and significantly — included in this restoration-salvation would be the gathering of the nations, who would also "go up to the mountain of the Lord, so that [they] may walk in his paths" (Mic 4:2).

Then it happened. Judgment came in the form of exile and the destruction of Jerusalem. Eventually a small remnant returned to the land, and hope sprang up that this would be it — the great day of Yahweh with the full blessings of his salvation. The restoration, however, turned out to be a colossal disappointment. The desert did not blossom like a rose; the nations did not gather at Jerusalem to honor Yahweh — indeed, only a minority of Jews did. The result was a long period of gloom in Israel's history as they eventually became a political pawn of the great powers — and many of God's people had become less than ardent Yahwists. It was a time when no prophetic voice was heard in the land, because there was no presence of the

THE TEXT AND THE LIFE OF THE CHURCH

Spirit[15] (who was by now understood to belong strictly to the final future day of the Lord[16]).

However, the hope for the future did not die. A group of writers emerged in Israel known as the apocalyptists,[17] who gave up on history as such, and looked for God to bring a crashing end to the present age, with its evil and oppression, and to usher in the Age to Come as an age of Spirit — an age of righteousness and justice.

It was into this kind of eschatological fervor that John the Baptist appeared announcing the nearness of the future. "Repent," he urged, "for the kingdom of God is near." "Get ready for the great coming day of the Lord" was his urgency. The Baptist's conviction was clearly proclaimed: the Messiah, though unrecognized, is already in our midst. Here was the return of the prophetic voice, and the people went out to hear with great anticipation. But the kingdom did not appear with John. Rather, he was arrested and eventually murdered. But soon after John's arrest news began to filter out of the synagogues in the north that another prophet had arisen who was announcing not simply the nearness of the kingdom, but the good news of the kingdom — that "the time was fulfilled; the kingdom of God was at hand." Indeed in his own home synagogue at Nazareth, Jesus announced that the great messianic prophecy of Isaiah 61, about the coming of God's "anointed one" who would proclaim the good news to the poor and the coming of the year of the Lord's favor, had in fact been fulfilled in his own coming (Luke 4:16-30).

What had been "fulfilled," according to Jesus, was that *in his own ministry* the time of God's favor toward "the poor" had come. In his healing the sick, casting out demons, and eating with sinners — and

---

15. See Jeremias, *New Testament Theology,* 80-82.

16. Thus, as Luke-Acts makes clear, such prophecies of the coming of the Spirit as Joel 2:28-32 (Acts 2:16-21) and Isaiah 61 (Luke 4:16-20) were understood totally eschatologically. The "quenched Spirit" would be poured out in abundance in the great coming Day of the Lord.

17. All of these writers wrote under the assumed name of an ancient worthy (e.g., Baruch, Enoch), probably because of their conviction that this was the time of the "quenched Spirit," who would reappear only at the end of the age, when the Spirit would once again be poured out — now "on all flesh."

thereby showing them God's unlimited mercy — the people were to understand that God's great eschatological day had finally dawned.

The Kingdom of God Is at Hand

This part of Jesus' announcement is the one that tends to create the most difficulty for moderns. How can the kingdom of God have become present with Jesus, given that everything is still topsy-turvy, that evil still abounds and injustice continues apace? How can the great climactic rule of God have come with him, since there has been such a long continuation of things, including human fallenness, since that coming?

The answer to these questions lies with the radical new thing Jesus himself did to the concept of God's rule: what he called "the mystery of the kingdom," he unfolded to his closest followers, but it was merely "parable" to those on the outside.[18]

The mystery had two parts to it, both of which had to do with the *presentness* of the kingdom in his own person and ministry: (1) that the great kingdom of the future had already begun with him; (2) that its coming was not "with great signs to be observed," but was present in weakness, in the humiliation of his incarnation.

1. As to the first matter, it is clear from the materials preserved in our Gospels that Jesus spoke of the kingdom of God as *both* a future event *and* a present reality. On one hand, there was still a future to the kingdom, which would come with power (Mark 9:1) when the Son of Man would come with the clouds of heaven (Mark 14:62). At that time the "great reversal" would take place. "The first *will be* last

---

18. See esp. Mark 4:10-12. What is difficult to translate into English is the play on the term "parable" in this saying, a term that in its Hebrew and Aramaic original covers the whole range of figurative and cryptic speech. Thus Jesus tells his disciples that he speaks in "parables" (= stories that unfold the nature of the kingdom as already present in his own ministry) so that they could understand; but to those on the outside they were merely "parables" (= puzzles) and nothing more. This saying, of course, refers especially to the "parables of the kingdom," not to the story parables, which are directed primarily toward the Pharisees. Their powerful point calls the Pharisees' actions into question before God in light of Jesus' own ministry.

and the last first," said Jesus (Mark 10:31); the poor, the hungry, and the weeping will trade places with the rich, well fed, and the laughing (Luke 6:20-25), and the outcasts will take their places at the great messianic banquet while the "children of the kingdom" will be thrown out (Matt 8:11-12 par.). There are scores of such texts in our gospels; indeed, were they the only texts, Jesus is at this point quite in keeping with the whole prophetic-apocalyptic tradition. There is a great coming day — the kingdom of God, he called it — when God will right the wrongs and settle the injustices.

But, of course, these are *not* the only texts, and with the others lay the uniqueness of Jesus' message and mission. "The kingdom is already at hand," he proclaimed, meaning not "near at hand" or simply "at the door," but actually in process of realization in his coming — and Jesus' own emphasis lay here. Thus he told the Pharisees that the kingdom was not coming (in the future is implied) "with great signs to be observed"; rather, the kingdom of God was *already* in their midst (Luke 17:20-21).[19] People were already "forcing their way" into it (Luke 16:16). In his eating at table with the outcasts, the great banquet of the future had already begun (Mark 2:19); and especially with Jesus' casting out demons and healing the sick, God's overthrow of Satan and his dominion was already taking place (Luke 11:20-21). God's stronger man had come, had bound the strong man, and was in process of spoiling his house (Mark 3:27). Already the great messianic prophecy of Isaiah 61 was being fulfilled, with its good news to the poor, freedom for prisoners, recovery of sight for the blind, and release of the oppressed (Luke 4:18-20). As we shall note in the next section, it is *the presentness of the kingdom in Jesus* that ultimately serves as the basis for the ongoing global mission of the church.

2. The presence of the kingdom in Jesus meant that the kingdom

---

19. Although there is some debate as to whether Jesus said that the kingdom is "within you" or "in your midst," the decisive considerations that Jesus was speaking to Pharisees and that he nowhere else so much as hints that the kingdom of God is some spiritual entity dwelling within human hearts make it certain that he said "in your midst." That, after all, is the point of the contrast — not with observable signs, but in his own person and ministry, which was of a kind radically different from their expectations.

of God was of a radically different order from people's expectations. Rather than representing the overthrow of the hated Roman Empire, it was present in weakness and suffering, where even the Son of Man had nowhere to lay his head (Luke 9:58), and where he came not to be served, but to serve and to give his life a ransom for the many (Mark 10:45). Thus the kingdom was like a seed growing quietly (Mark 4:26-29), like a minuscule mustard seed, whose beginnings were so small and insignificant that nothing could be expected of it, but whose final end — inherent in the seed itself and therefore inevitable — would be an herb of such dimensions that birds could rest in its branches (Matt 13:31-32).

What becomes clear from all this, therefore, is that for Jesus himself the kingdom of God was both "already" and "not yet"; it was both "now" and "yet to come." It was "now" with his own invasion of Satan's turf and the spoiling of his house. With the coming of Jesus the kingdom of God has already been inaugurated; it has already penetrated the present. But inherent in its presence with Jesus was likewise its final and full consummation with the future coming of the Son of Man. The future is not something new, it is merely the consummation of what Jesus already began through his ministry, and finally and especially through his death, resurrection, and the gift of the Spirit. Thus, the kingdom, though still future, is already "at hand."

Repent and Believe the Good News

These final words of Mark's summary represent the human response to the coming of the kingdom with Jesus. They speak of the kingdom in its relationship to the human condition. As it comes to overthrow the old order, it requires repentance. As it puts in motion the setting in of the new, it is good news to be believed. It is also clear that in Jesus' own teaching, however, this twofold response takes place in reverse order. That is, one does not repent in order to gain entrance to the kingdom; rather, the kingdom is God's gift (Luke 12:32), present in Jesus himself, which is the good news that leads to repentance.

Thus Jesus especially announces the kingdom as "good news to the poor" (Luke 4:18), so much so that when the imprisoned John, out of his own uncertainty, inquires about Jesus (after all, Jesus hardly fit the categories set up by John's preaching!), Jesus once again uses this language from Isaiah 61 as the authentication of his messiahship (Matt 11:5).

But who indeed are "the poor" who are the recipients of the good news of the kingdom?[20] For Jesus they clearly include the traditional "poor" (the widows and orphans, who represent all the helpless and defenseless, to whom God has committed himself and his people to plead their cause). His concern for the helpless, found both in his ministry and his parables,[21] makes it clear that "the poor" still include such people. But for Jesus they also include that other great class of "poor," the "sinners" — those who recognize themselves as impoverished of spirit (Matt 5:3) and who stand helpless before God, in need of his mercy. They are thus represented in the prodigal, who "comes to himself" and receives his father's warm embrace (Luke 15:11-32); in the town "sinner," who weeps over Jesus' feet and receives his word of forgiveness (Luke 7:36-50); in the wretched tax-collector, whose gracious acceptance by Jesus leads to his giving back all and more of what he had stolen (Luke 19:1-10). They are those who have been wearied by the heavy yoke of sin and the pharisaic burden of law, who are invited by Jesus to come to him and change yokes, because his yoke is easy and his burden light (Matt 11:28-30).

This is the good news of the kingdom. The year of God's favor

---

20. For discussions of this matter, see Jeremias, *New Testament Theology*, pp. 109-13; and the entries in *TDNT* on "gospel" by G. Friedrich (2:707-37) and on "tax collector" by O. Michel (8:88-106). For recent discussions see the articles by Donald E. Gowan (OT) and Bruce J. Malina (NT) in *Interpretation* 41 (1987): 341-67.

21. Thus he heals the only son of a widow (Luke 7:11-15) and commends another widow for her large-heartedness (Mark 12:41-44); he shows compassion on lepers by healing them (Mark 1:40-45; Luke 17:11-19); and he urges the "haves" to give away their riches to help the "have-nots" (Mark 10:21; Luke 12:33) and to invite only the poor, the crippled, the lame, and the blind to their banquets (Luke 14:12-14). In his parables in particular he singles out the needy as the special recipients of God's gracious provision (Luke 16:19-31; 14:15-24).

has come. With Jesus there is forgiveness for all; the poor and beggars are summoned to the banquet; the door of the Father's house stands open; people who work but an hour receive a full day's pay, because the landowner is generous. God's rule has become present in Jesus to free people from *all* the tyrannies of Satan's rule, to bring "release to the captives" in every imaginable way, including those who have been encumbered by the pharisaic understanding of the law.

Such good news thus leads to repentance. Jesus does not tell Zacchaeus to repent and then he will eat with him; rather his gracious acceptance of Zacchaeus in all his ugliness led to the latter's repentance. A woman caught in adultery is freely forgiven, and then told to go and sin no more.

Repentance for Jesus is thus not simply remorse. It means to become as a child, to humble oneself and become totally dependent on one's heavenly Father (Matt 18:4). It means to lose one's life, and thereby to find it again — because one has been "found" by God himself (Mark 8:35). But it also means to enter into discipleship, to deny one's very self, to take up a cross — the place of self-sacrifice on behalf of others — and thus to follow Jesus himself (Mark 8:34).

Therefore, the gift of the kingdom means to become a child of the king, who as it turns out is also one's heavenly Father. Such children are not to worry; the Father has committed himself to their care and provision of needs (Matt 6:25-34). They in turn are to become like the Father and are expected to be his salt and light in the world by living out the life of the future — the kingdom of God itself — in the present age. Thus the ethics of the kingdom are not some new, intensive form of law. They, too, are gift. They reflect the righteousness of the kingdom of God that "goes beyond that of the Pharisees" (Matt 5:20). As God is perfect, so his children are invited to share his likeness in the fallen world as it awaits the final consummation (Matt 5:38). Forgiven, they forgive; recipients of mercy, they show mercy; beneficiaries of abundant grace in every way, they bring others to become beneficiaries as well by showing them abundant grace.

Such is the kingdom of God in the mission and message of Jesus. Though veiled in the weakness and suffering of his own incarnation

173

and subsequent death on the cross, it has come with power — the real thing — in the form of life-changing acceptance and forgiveness, destroying the power of Satan in every way. "I saw Satan fall from heaven," Jesus says after the Seventy-two return from a mission of casting out demons (Luke 10:18). Satan's rule is on its way out; its stranglehold on humanity in every form — sin, sickness, oppression, possession, injustice — has received its deathblow in the life and ministry of Jesus, and especially in his death and resurrection. And such is the foundation for the global mission of the church in our own day.

THE KINGDOM OF GOD
AND OUR GLOBAL MISSION

It does not take too much further reflection to see how relevant — and crucial — Jesus' message and ministry are to the total global mission of the church. If Jesus for the most part limited his ministry to the Jews of his own historical context, our own task is to bring the good news of the kingdom to our own historical context — our global village, the world. There are several ways in which this is so, flowing directly out of the mission and message of Jesus himself.

The "Fulfilled Time"

Although Jesus himself does not refer to the covenant with Abraham, the covenant with its blessing for the nations was inherent in the prophetic message that Jesus announced as "fulfilled." This point in particular is picked up by the Apostle Paul as the crucial element in his own understanding of the Gentile mission.[22] But such "fulfillment" is already inherent in Jesus' own proclamation. What was being fulfilled was the coming of the day of salvation that the

---

22. See especially the argument of Gal 3:1-18, in which Paul actually cites the covenantal promise from Gen 12:3, but in the language of Gen 18:18, so as to include "all nations" (i.e., "all the Gentiles"; 3:8).

prophets had announced; and included in their announcement, especially in Isaiah, was the coming of the Servant of the Lord, of whom Yahweh had said, "I will also make you a light for the Gentiles, that you may bring my salvation to the ends of the earth" (Isa 49:6; cf. 42:6). This is the very theme that Simeon in particular enunciated as he held in his arms the child who was to be "the consolation of Israel" (Luke 2:32). Jesus himself expresses the fulfillment of this theme in more indirect ways, but there can be little question that herein lies the foundation for our global mission.

One of the seldom noted motifs in the ministry of Jesus is his taking on himself the role of the Servant of Yahweh, as articulated in Isaiah 42–53 (which also extends to include Isaiah 61, even though "servant" language is not found expressly in that passage).[23] In Isaiah the "servant" is alternatively Israel collectively understood and Israel represented by the one Spirit-anointed servant, who would redeem Israel and the nations. Surely it is no accident that Jesus also seems to fill *both* of these roles.

On the one hand, after his baptism *in water,* Jesus was *tested forty* days and nights *in the desert.* He overcame Satan, it should be noted, by citing passages from Deuteronomy, taken from the very places where Israel, after going through the *water* of the Red Sea, spent *forty* years *in the desert* and failed the *test.* Early on Jesus gathered twelve disciples about him, as one who consciously stepped into the role of Israel itself. Furthermore, in Luke's version of the Transfiguration (9:31), Jesus is seen talking to Moses (= the Law) and Elijah (= the Prophets) about the *exodus*[24] he would "fulfill" in Jerusalem. Even though he does not interpret it frequently, when he does, in Mark 10:45 ("the Son of Man 'serves' by giving his life as a ransom for the many") and in the words of institution at the Last Supper (Luke 22:20), he consciously does so in the language both of Isaiah

23. See, e.g., how Isa 61:1-2 expressly picks up the language of the first of the "servant songs" in 42:7.

24. This is Luke's actual word; because it seems to make so little sense, English translators invariably turn it into something like his "departure" (NIV) or "passing" (JB). But by using this Greek word, Luke clearly understands it to mean far more than simply death or "departure." In his death Jesus effects the new exodus, the new salvation for the people of God.

53 (esp. vv. 11-12) and of Jeremiah 31 (the new covenant). Thus God's servant "Israel" in turn becomes the one servant *for* Israel, who will give his life for Israel and through his poured-out blood establish the new covenant with Israel. What is significant for our purposes is that deeply imbedded in the servant passages that Jesus sees as being fulfilled in himself is salvation for the Gentiles as well.

Thus his announcement of the kingdom as "the fulfilled time" means not simply that he ushered in the end of the present age — that he did indeed — but also that he brought to fulfillment the covenant with Abraham, as further reflected in the prophets, that God would bless the nations through him. This of course is exactly the point Paul makes, defending a law-free Gentile mission, when he argues as a Christian "rabbi" that the repeated phrase in the Abrahamic covenant, "and to his seed," does not refer to many, but to one true "seed," Jesus Christ himself, through whom the promise, the blessing of the nations, was fulfilled by the coming of the Spirit (Gal 3:1-4:7).

Our own global mission, therefore, is deeply woven into the biblical understanding of Jesus' death and resurrection for all people (see esp. 1 Tim 2:4-6), as that understanding is rooted first of all in the teaching of Jesus himself. His giving his own life "for many" means "for the great and numberless many" (reflecting Isa 53:11-12), who will hear it as good news and respond with repentance. The proclamation of that good news, of course, is what the ongoing mission of the church is all about.

The Kingdom as "Now" and "Not Yet"

The eschatological framework of the kingdom as both "now" and "not yet" provides further theological basis for our global mission. On the one hand, the "now" of the kingdom as "good news to the poor" is the underlying premise of our entire understanding of the ministry of Jesus: it is thus also the inherent imperative of the kingdom until the final consummation. The proclamation of the good news of the kingdom lies at the heart of everything Jesus said and did; this is the "kingdom proclamation" that he inaugurated.

At the same time, and on the other hand, the fact that the kingdom is still "not yet" does not mean that we simply await God's completion of what Jesus began. To the contrary, it means that the inaugurated kingdom, the good news of salvation for all that Jesus proclaimed, must be further proclaimed to all "the poor" in every place. This is precisely the intent of Jesus' own word that "this gospel [good news] of the kingdom will be preached in the whole world as a testimony to all nations, and then the end will come" (Matt 24:14). And this is turn is the reason for the Great Commission given to his disciples by the Risen Lord, to "go and make disciples of all nations" (Matt 28:19).

Our present existence, therefore, is one that is lived out "between the times" — between the beginning and the conclusion of the End. The final consummation, our glorious future, has been guaranteed for us by the death and resurrection of our Lord. But meanwhile, until that future has come in its fullness, we are to be the people of the future in the present age, who continue the proclamation of the kingdom as good news to the poor.

The Kingdom as "Good News for the Poor"

A further implication for the global mission of the church rests with Jesus' announcement of the kingdom as good news *for the poor*. We noted earlier that this includes both the traditional "poor" of the OT (especially the helpless and defenseless) and the "poor" in the larger sense of all who stand "impoverished in spirit" in the presence of the eternal God, and thus become recipients of his grace and mercy. The beatitudes in Luke 6:20-21 and Matt 5:3-10 capture these two emphases respectively. The tragedy of much subsequent church history is its tendency to function with a half canon (either Luke's or Matthew's version) with regard to these congratulatory words of Jesus. For some "the poor" are only the "spiritually" so, the sinners; for others, usually in reaction to the former, "the poor" tend to become only the economically deprived. This unfortunate bifurcation quite misses the ministry of Jesus himself.

The OT basis for this language, of course, comes especially from the law, with the expressions of God's concern for the helpless, lest they be either neglected, or worse, taken advantage of by the rest. In a more agrarian society, the "poor" are especially so with regard to the land. Thus, especially in Deuteronomy, they include both the obvious helpless — the widows and orphans — and the Levites and aliens as well, precisely because they had no direct access to ownership of land. Thus throughout the entire OT, true piety is expressed in terms of pleading the cause of the poor (see the magnificent expressions of this in Job 29:7-17; 31:5-8; 13:23), and unrighteousness is denounced in similar terms (see Amos, Isa 58). But at the same time, especially in the Psalms, the "poor" are those who suffer misfortune of every kind, and include both the oppressed (Psa 9) and those who before God are conscious of their sins (Pss 32 and 51).

When Jesus, therefore, announced good news to the poor, his proclamation was for those who were needy in every sense of the term. What is significant for our present concern are two items: First, our gospel is not simply that of "saving souls"; it is rather, as with Jesus, the bringing of wholeness to broken people in every kind of distress. Mission simply cannot be divided between "spiritual" and "physical." To do one is to do the other, and both constitute the global mission of the church.

Second, and especially is this so in Luke's Gospel, the "poor" to whom Jesus comes are represented by every kind of first-century outcast — the traditional poor, sinners, Samaritans, Gentiles, and women. Luke, himself a Gentile, had come to recognize that the heart of ministry of Jesus was "salvation for all." In his Gospel he especially included those narratives that illustrated the total "cross-section" of society to whom Jesus came. In the Acts, by focusing on the Gentile mission, he demonstrated that it was God's intent through the Holy Spirit to take that salvation to the ends of the earth. Such an understanding, Luke saw clearly, was absolutely central to the ministry of Jesus himself.

Our global mission, therefore, is rooted ultimately in Jesus' application of Isaiah 53 and 61:1-2 to himself. He himself brought in the time of the End, the "year of the Lord's favor," in which the good news to the poor meant release for the captives of all kinds. He was anointed by the Holy Spirit precisely for such a mission; and he in turn poured out the Spirit on his disciples so that they might continue that same mission.

The Spirit and the Kingdom

Finally, one further aspect of the kingdom and our global mission needs to be noted, especially in a book designed in part to give a biblical rationale for Pentecostal missions, and that is the role of the Spirit in the kingdom. Here again, we are especially indebted to Luke's presentation of the good news. For he makes it clear that both the Savior himself and his followers are empowered for the life and ministry of the kingdom by the Holy Spirit. Especially in his Gospel, Luke singles out the Spirit as the power for Jesus' life and mission;[25] and it is by that same Spirit that he ties together his Gospel and Acts[26] in terms of the ongoing proclamation of good news to the poor — and thus to the ends of the earth.

As with them, so with ourselves. The kingdom has come; it is still to come. With Jesus the time of the future, the day of salvation, has been inaugurated. But the empowering was the work of the Holy

25. Not only is Jesus conceived of the Holy Spirit (Luke 1:35), but his entire earthly ministry is lived out by the power of the Spirit. The Holy Spirit descends on him at his baptism (3:21-22); he is led by the Spirit into the desert for the time of testing (4:1); he returns from the desert into Galilee in the power of the Spirit (4:14); and it was in the "power of the Lord" that he healed the sick (5:17). Consistent with this picture, in Peter's speech to Cornelius' household, "God anointed Jesus of Nazareth with the Holy Spirit and power, and he went around doing good and healing all who were under the power of the devil, because God was with him" (Acts 10:38).

26. See, e.g., the conclusion of the Gospel (24:45-49), where their ongoing proclamation of the good news of forgiveness for all the nations is to be accomplished by Jesus' sending them "what the Father has promised," namely, "power from on high." This in turn is where the story of Acts begins — with the repeated promise of the Spirit, so that they will bear witness to the nations (Acts 1:1-11), followed by the narrative of the outpoured Spirit (2:1-41), which concludes with the promise of the Spirit for "all who are far off — for all whom the Lord our God will call" (v. 39). Note especially Acts 1:1-5, where this ministry is specifically tied to "all that Jesus *began* to do and to teach."

Spirit. What Jesus began "both to do and say" is now the ministry he has left his church until he comes again. The mission is that of Jesus himself — God's kingdom as having come as good news for the poor. But the empowering for the kingdom, as then, is the continuing work of the Spirit. May God help us by his Spirit both to will and to do of his good pleasure — salvation for all through Christ.